FILICIDE
NOTES ON NARCISSISM

Carmem Dametto
Translation Rafa Lombardino

FILICIDE
NOTES ON NARCISSISM

1st Edition
POD

Petrópolis
KBR
2013

Translation **Rafa Lombardino**
Text Edition **Noga Sklar**
Cover **"The Sacrifice of Isaac" by Caravaggio, oil on
canvas,** *circa* **1603**

ISBN: 978-85-8180-168-1

KBR Editora Digital Ltda.
www.kbrdigital.com.br
atendimento@kbrdigital.com.br
55|24|2222.3491

PSY000000 - Psychology

Printed in USA

Carmem Dametto is a psychiatrist and psychoanalyst with the Brazilian Psychoanalysis Society - Rio de Janeiro Branch (SBPRJ). She was born in Garibaldi, State of Rio Grande do Sul, in 1941 and has been living in Rio de Janeiro since the 1970s. She was persecuted during the Military Dictatorship in Brazil because of her Marxist background. Perhaps it is due to her line of reasoning that she has been able to implement an innovative therapeutic approach with her patients. She has written five books and co-founded the former "Margaridas" Protected Hostel, which was a dynamic clinic with in-patients that also worked as half-way house. She was a Full Professor of Psychiatry in Vassouras and Chief Supervisor at the first dynamic treatment clinic "Vila Pinheiros," open in Rio de Janeiro in the 1970s.

Email: carmemdametto@gmail.com
Author's blog: carmemdametto.blogspot.com

To my colleagues in psychotherapy: psychologists,
psychiatrists, and psychoanalysts

"(...) the difficulty that a man has dying without a son to imaginatively kill and to survive him, thus providing the only continuity that men know."
D.W. Winnicott

Acknowledgements

There is always a team behind a piece of literary work.

Psychologist Patrícia A. Calhau worked to prevent the filicide of *Filicide* from its inception, around 1989, until its final stages.

Psychologists Maria Antônia Rocha e Silva and Rosa Maria Saraiva recognized and celebrated it since its birth, when it was only a draft.

Author and psychiatrist Carmine Martuscello needs no introduction; his beautiful preface speaks for itself.

Later, Professor of Classic Literature Lygia Fontfer Martins took care of it without, however, altering the original style.

To everybody, *Filicide* is eternally grateful.

Table of Contents

Acknowledgements • 11

Cântico Negro [Dark Chant] • 15

Preface • 19

Author's note • 25

Introduction • 27

Taboo in Psychological
    Treatment • 31

Oedipus at the Crossroads • 45

Narcissism • 59

Filicide • 81

Forms of Filicide • 97

Creating an Affective Bond • 117

On Therapists and Therapies • 133

Symbiosis and Narcissism • 153

Filicide: A Constant in Human
    History • 163

Omnipotence vs. Impotence in
    Psychosis • 175

Oedipus Complex vs. Depressive
    Position • 179

Possible Traces of Life in Utero as Seen
    in Psychosis • 181

Final Considerations • 187

Bibliographical References • 189

CÂNTICO NEGRO [DARK CHANT][1]

"Come this way,"
Some tell me with sweet eyes,
Reaching out their arms,
Certain that it would do me good
To listen when they tell me
"Come, come this way."
I look at them with weary eyes;
There is irony and exhaustion in my eyes.
I cross my arms,
And never go that way.
This is my glory:
To create inhumanity,
Follow no one.
I live with the same unwillingness

---

1 Written by José Régio, Vinícius de Moraes, Luis Carlos Lacerda, and Clarice Lispector. The text was transcribed from the Brazilian singer and interpreter Maria Bethânia's "Nossos Momentos" and the verses may not correspond to those of the original poem. It was transcribed as I have experienced, since it's very hard and personal to keep up with the way Maria Bethânia recites it in her unique way. She doesn't recite the text in the rhythm they were written, but in the way she feels it.

With which I used to tear at my mother's womb.
No, I will not go that way.
I'll only go where my own steps take me.
None of you has answers to what puzzles me.
You only repeat, "Come, come this way."
I'd rather slip in muddy alleys,
Swirl as a rag in the wind,
Drag my bloody feet,
But I will not go that way.
If I came into this world
It was only to deflower virgin forests
And leave footprints on unexplored sands.
The harder you try, the more you'll fail.
How could you be the ones
Who'll hand me axes, tools, and valor
To overcome my own obstacles?
In your veins runs
The blood of our flimsy forefathers.
And you love that which comes easy.
I love the distance and the mirage.
I love the abyss, the flood, and the desert.
Go! You have your roads, your treaties,
Your philosophers, your great thinkers!
I have my insanity,
And I raise it as a torch
Burning in the dark of night.
And I feel the foam and the blood,
I hear the chanting lips.
God and the Devil guide me;
No one else will do.
We all had a father;

We all had a mother.
Whereas I never begin,
Nor do I end;
I'm the offspring of love and hate.
Oh, shall no one show me
Compassionate intentions.
Shall no one ask me for definitions.
Shall no one say,
"Come this way."
My life is a windstorm ignited,
It's a wave sighted,
It's an extra atom excited.
I do not know which way to go.
I do not know to where I am going.
But I do know I will not go that way.

Preface

I shall start by disclosing that this is a book of utmost importance to the study of filicide. Rather, it is fundamental. As a mental phenomenon present in the deepest unconscious mind of human beings, filicide behavior must obviously be detected before its destructive potential can ever be fulfilled—not to mention the psychotic condition in which this phenomenon appears more evidently. Those who wish to include family members in their professional scope must be familiar with it and understand it well, resorting to truly therapeutic intentions before they can ever be considered competent enough to address such a complicated human ensemble formed by parents and children acting affectionately towards one another.

Carmem Dametto, who also penned another book on theories and techniques for treating psychosis, shows us how we can learn (and teach) with practical and clinical exercise while experiencing the daily lives of psychotic patients and their families. It is with the use of her techniques during routine interactions that she grasps the theory and transforms it into unique books. This one, once again, confirms one of her originalities. She does not renounce to the familiar tone of someone who is having a conversation, simplifying each discovery without the need to create a mysterious atmosphere in order to monopolize knowledge.

Filicide is yet to be thoroughly explored in psychoanalysis theory. Maybe it is because this clinical condition is more difficult to detect, because those who should identify it have some blind spots when it comes to the subject. Maybe it is due to the fact that it is considered taboo, for it clashes with the main theme that is preferred by ruling authorities who surround the "official" psychoanalytic knowledge with red tape. The thing is that parricide remains in the spotlight of core theories about Oedipus in the vast majority of publications on this matter. Despite lacking resources to address the breadth and wealth of psychological events involving the affection that flows within a family, there is a stubborn resistance to acknowledging what happens to the parent component in a family setting.

With this book, Carmem Dametto corrects this mistake and contributes to giving a more realistic and efficient focus to family therapy by attributing a true psychopathological potential to filicide. Her professional experience with psychotic patients puts her in the ideal position to teach the subject and keep an accurate perspective of unconscious events as they are unveiled in pathologies of this nature, that is, exposed with maximum intensity. That is how she finds her clinical examples, which become great learning experiences on how to work with patients once filicide is observed in parents. Thus is one of the great merits of this book: It is practical and objective, without measuring words to tell it like it is. Her objectivity is the same, both with patients and with readers.

Another unprecedented and very interesting point is that, besides being fundamental to the correct understanding of the Oedipus Complex in human narcissistic behavior, this book also shifts the focus to filicide to show evidence of similarities between the myths of Oedipus and Narcissus. Psychoanalysis is applied here in reading the myths to show that the same filicide conduct present in Oedipus is also found in Narcissus. The mythological meanings of these two Greek classics are explored in a way that no other psychoanalyst ever attempted before. In my opinion, this fact in and of itself justifies this book, for it opens up a new horizon to all human tragedies. That is how we can better understand Man's psychological nature and see him as a being who, deep down in his soul, preserves levels of narcissism that are potentially filicidal. When filicide and narcissism—and, consequently, many more other elements of psychosis—are brought together to be understood in this manner, they are no longer only abstract, theoretical concepts; they are seen as concrete data on a patient's life experiences and become clearer to a therapist's perception, potentially being transformed into words that will promote a cure.

Going through the text, readers will have this clairvoyance feeling, as if they were in contact with elementary knowledge, accessing truths that have always existed, but until now had remained hidden from their conscious mind due to their impossibility to think about what has been repressed for centuries of acculturation. If the

Greek mythology unveiled here has contributed to support what clinical observation had already revealed, we would confirm once more the potential that time has to consolidate facts and events in the human mind, as they are manifested in current times, that will demand specific arrangements in order to revert any negative consequences. These arrangements represent therapeutic practices, backed by a set of theoretical tools that include the knowledge provided by revelations such as these, about the history of human culture and its millenarian assimilation of filicide as an unconscious baggage.

As we read and think about it, we feel that filicide is something so obvious and palpable that it makes us wonder why it has been drown out and excluded from the psychoanalytical debate. To paraphrase Caetano Veloso, whose song is quoted in the book, something is to be revealed and it will surprise everyone "due to the fact that is has always been hidden, despite being obvious." For emphasis, if Nelson Rodrigues could voice his opinion, he would say it is "howling obvious." And so it is. Truth is usually obvious. And simple. This is what we find in this book. The great truth is revealed before our eyes as something elementary and easy to assimilate, exactly as the best insightful moments during psychoanalytical efforts in search of a cure.

During family therapy, psychoanalytical treatment, psychotherapy sessions with patients in general, or simply a healthy life, we are required to be introspective about a series of elements in our family and love life. Our feelings and thoughts need something or someone to work as a mental propeller capable of promoting innovative change. I can personally attest to the fact that Carmem Dametto is one of those people with the constructive ability to touch us deeply where we are most uncomfortable, limited, or suffering while yearning for something good to happen. This is what I feel in my personal relationship with her. And such is the feeling I get from reading her works. Before I met her, I had known her from her books; they drove me to look for her in order to keep studying and learning. That is exactly what I did and I'm better for that. I was also driven to write a few books and go on improving my work method.

I am sure that this sincerely thankful testimony will be understood by those who are now reading it. And I hope it will be an example for those who wish to learn more and put what they have learned to use in a clear and objective manner.

Without further ado, I shall now give you, the readers, an opportunity to start—or continue—reading this text and go through the productive thinking and learning process that Carmem Dametto's experience has to offer.

Carmine Martuscello

Author's note

The following explanation is targeted at laypersons reading this book, since it was basically written with therapists in mind.

Filicide, whether it is pathological or not, is an inherent feeling to human nature. When I deal with the subject, it is not my intention to denounce or criticize the parents and children of patients or regular people; I do so to understand a universal phenomenon from which many run away upon considering it something "wrong." Actually, it is not something wrong. Those who say they have never thought or committed filicide in a certain way would be lying or have failed to find room inside themselves to experience it. We all, parents and children, feel or withstand filicide of a pathological nature or otherwise. It happens unconsciously, whether we are the victims or perpetrators. However, it bears repeating: It is something as physiological as peeing. And, as such, it must be talked about and treated the same way.

This book was conceived in 1989 and completed

in April 1994 with three chapters adapted from some of my previous books.

Carmem Dametto

INTRODUCTION

The purpose of this book is to exhibit and basically explain what I was able to perceive and understand from **filicide** and **narcissism** during my clinical experiences in treating psychotic patients and their families. Here, I will transcribe my hypothesis and work method for dealing with feelings and behaviors, which may be merely mental or effectively materialized, involving psychotic patients and their families in regards to filicide and narcissism.

In his book *O Assassinato dos filhos (filicídio) [Murdering Sons and Daughters (Filicide)]*, Arnaldo Rascovsky goes deep into the subject in a broader fashion. The following authors also talk about **filicide**: Grinberg did a magnificent job through Freud's *Totem and Taboo*, and Tractenberg, with *Psicanálise da Circuncisão* [Psychoanalysis of Circumcision].

This book was born out of necessity to show the deep severity of this disorder in a psychotic patient, at a moment in time when Brazilian policies on mental illnesses have suddenly and absurdly decided to abolish the very existence of the disease. There are only cases of brief admission in the public sector; and those considered too lengthy, therefore inadequate, [2]are restricted to the so-called classic hospitals. Only outpatient treatment remains, even though it only exists in theory.[3] As omnipotent beings, therapists and politicians narcissistically decreed the non-existence or the low severity of this mental illness and all the suffering it brings not only to patients, but to their family members as well.

Unlike the Eastern Civilization that has always seen it as any other disease, I believe Western Civilization has spent centuries "marinating" this mental disorder and, now, all of a sudden, has been trying to demystify it in the past two or three decades. Well, it is now an impossible leap. It would take centuries for people who have been afraid of schizophrenia to see it as something natural. I was raised in an environment in which madness was not mystified.[4] Consequently, I understand that mental disorders are not the end of the world. But I also understand that it is still perceived as something extremely severe, since our culture has been frightening people for hundreds of years with its manifestations. Filicide is one of them, as it falls into this category.

Seventy-four percent of children born in northeast Brazil die before they turn five years old.[5] Isn't it significant? How come nobody tries to understand the

---

2 They don't offer any treatment that could lead to a cure.

3 In the best-case scenario, appointments are made for patients to "miraculously" see a psychiatrist every two months.

4 Cf. DAMETTO, Carmem. *Loucura: Mitos e Realidade*. Petrópolis: KBR, 2012.

5 Editor's note: The information is from the original edition (1994).

reason why we continue to elect politicians who take the budget reserved to end hunger and malnutrition and use it to their own benefit or that of their friends? Are we all filicidal? No, we are all conniving at filicide in Brazil, which has now become true genocide. And why is that? Why do we allow patients with AIDS to die? It is not because of a lack of funds coming from abroad or raised within the country! Right now, we allow those afflicted by cholera to die. The next in line will certainly be the mad ones; suicidal individuals will be deprived of admission for treatment and outpatient care will be denied to those who are not suicidal. We will repeat the unfortunate spectacle seen in Italy. However, as health care providers, if we are able to observe and understand the severity of this process, we will be able to make a contribution to preventing the aggravation, the consumption of mass filicide by the State. That was my intention when writing this book.

Taboo in Psychological Treatment

I have noticed that a basic feeling such as filicide is extremely common in psychiatric and psychoanalytic clinical assessments; nevertheless, it has not been given proper attention, care, and emphasis by theorists. Both **filicide** and **narcissism** exist in *every* person, whether they are healthy or ill, but these conditions are denied by those who work with the emotionally afflicted. The thing is that narcissism and filicide are two of the most primitive emotions in humans. However, when they are not identified and properly treated, patients are similar to a building whose construction started on the third floor. Denying these feelings that have become taboo in Western Society comes as a result of their being extremely painful, both for therapists and patients. That is how everybody makes an unconscious pact no to touch the subject. Still, individuals who are ill might suffer in solitude when these emotions surface to their conscious mind.

In addition to finding the theme of "filicide" in Rascovsky, Tractenberg, and Grinberg, implicitly explored in common literature and, naturally, in Freud's works, there may be other books I am unaware of and I hereby apologize.

Freud went deeper into other taboos: Incest and parricide. He also touched narcissism, but did not address the filicide that comes hand-in-hand with it.

Anyway, since these issues are part of my daily routine, I felt compelled to write about them and narrate some clinical examples. However, for readers to better understand my drive, I believe it is important for them to learn more about my personal and professional background.

The way I deal with my patients—be it during outpatient treatment or hospitalization—has already been addressed in small sections of my other books. I am certain that it mostly comes from my cultural and family background, my psychoanalytical treatment, and my continuous 34-year experience with hospitalized patients and, concomitantly, 27-year miscellaneous outpatient treatment, starting with my six years of higher education (Full Professor of Psychiatry) and supervision of health care professionals.

This is the result of my long journey, my presentations at Congresses and Conferences throughout Brazil and at the three institutions I help to found and for which I acted as General Supervisor; developing courses mainly on the clinical issue of Psychosis at colleges or privately; teaching psychiatric and psychoanalytical comprehension through the books I have published and the magazines I helped to create, and during the eight years I participated in Assistance to Psychotic Patient Symposium events under the auspices of the Psychiatric Association of Rio de Janeiro.

The way I work is also closely related to my dynamic eight-year academic career in Psychiatry and my five-year analytical studies. I should also emphasize the fact that I have rarely been the first therapist seen by my patients. Most of them have had a long psychiatric and/or psychotherapeutic and/or psychoanalytical and/or pharmacological experience, all of which had failed. Consequently, I am their "last resort" and they come to see me at different times in their lives, hoping to live a better life. It so happens that I use my own treatment, which is the result of who I am, of my life's journey, and I have found strong support for it after reading Freud himself describe the "Schreber Case," which opened up many doors to understanding psychosis. He once said that we must continue to always seek a new way to treat those he refers to as "narcissistic patients."

Where and How I was Raised

I was born in Garibaldi, a small village in an Italian settlement located in the State of Rio Grande do Sul. In 1941, during World War II, an Italian dialect was the only language spoken there. My contact with the Portuguese language came with the catechism they forced me to study. I ended up memorizing it by ear, which is what I did with all the books from elementary school. Evidently, after memorizing everything, I was able to write perfectly in Portuguese. I graduated from elementary school as the head of the class and had to recite Castro Alves at every celebration organized by the rural school I attended. And I'd recite: "Oh, what skies, what land, what sea"—and I only got to see the sea at age eleven, in Porto Alegre.

Family

We are five children. My parents were merchants, from a family of merchants. On my Dad's side, the Damettos, they were all merchants; on my Mom's side, the Caselanis, they were all merchants. We were lucky that they had us children working from an early age, as farmers used to do. There were about thirty families in the village, approximately two or three hundred people in the settlement. I say we were "lucky" because working was a *right*, not an *obligation*. It was only during my contact with the middle-class Brazilian culture in Porto Alegre that I became aware of work as a terrible *obligation*. Even though we were living in the end of the world, my parents never stopped reading the paper or listening to the radio, and that was how they provided us with a different cultural background, a better one than that of settlers in general.

My academic career in Medicine, Psychiatry, and Psychoanalysis is a direct reflection of my primary worldview. My first impressions and feelings, my attempts at "acculturation," were developed and matured in a very difficult way. I can say that, to this day, at fifty-two years of age, I have not gone through a complete "acculturation." My roots are predominantly present in everything I did, do, learned, and learn.

My professional life is completely dedicated to understanding and treating psychotic individuals. The elaboration of certain theories and concepts that I use have arisen of theoretical works by Freud and other authors. However, they are a result of my own life's journey, my clinical work, my own suffering and experiences in adult life and, mainly, my childhood and the "childhood" that I relived in therapy sessions.

When I was a child, the Korean War terrorized me. Upon hearing the intro to "Esso Reporter" on the radio, I'd start to panic. In the concrete thoughts of my six- or seven-year-old self, I imagined Korea as a place that was right around the bend, following the road that would lead to another village, and that soon U.S. bombs would fall over our heads. I had a notion of time and space that was very inflexible and painful, which has led me to have an anti-American feeling to this day—and it has been enhanced by the Americans repeating what they did and do in other countries.

All psychoanalysts must have gone through similar experiences. I just don't know if they give it the same importance I did, which later I had to perceive as "my internal Korea." Much like the other one, this Korea went through a foreign intervention as well—that of the therapist—but it actually united the two sides that had been fighting inside of me. I imagine this is what all my therapist colleagues had to do in order to learn about themselves and that, while playing the role of patient-therapists, they may have had a chance to reveal themselves, without holding back, to a good therapist who knew how to "take a dive" with them in an unexplored sea, bringing them back to safety at the shore, thus avoiding the creation of a false self, which is the biggest problem of many patients who go through therapy and still need another true treatment. At least, that is what I have seen in clinical practice.

As I learned with my people, and it bears repeating, working was a *right*, not an *obligation*. In fact, working—rather than employment—has a fundamental value to human life and, above all, to recovery for a psychotic patient. Occupational therapists must have a clear notion of how important it is for patients to work as a way to start reformulating their ego. Unfortunately, even therapists and psychiatrists refer patients to occupational therapy only as a way to help them do something with their time, not as a way to mature their ego and/or seek personal satisfaction, whether they are ill or healthy.

I would like to mention a patient who had delusions about being a great painter. If she had such delusion, she unconsciously knew that she had the ability to be it. However, externalizing it sounded like a delirious idea. It was my job to give her paper and a pencil and hope that, one day, this "delirious" idea manifested itself as something normal. My patient started to work on drafts and wound up being a great painter indeed. What could this "delirious idea" be? Maybe it was the fact that she consciously could not stand being aware of her ability and the consequences that it would bring to her new adult life if she acknowledged herself as a person. Of course, her treatment went through very serious stages, in which her enormous narcissism would show, as well as the filicide attempts she had suffered. Her father, an artist, had some-how prevented one of his children to follow in his foot-steps. After seven years of intense therapy, "diving and going back to shore," the patient was able to restructure herself and become a whole person to lead a happy life.

This patient in particular was never hospitalized, despite the deep suicidal feelings that tormented her for years. She did not need to be hospitalized because she had a family holding environment to support her. She did not need the holding environment available at our hospital (half-way house[6]), which is something that unfortunate-ly is not available at other hospitals. Our patients can go outside to work, study, and lead normal lives, but cannot live at home with their family due to the absence of cer-tain conditions that they need to live. When a patient be-comes "their own father and mother," as another one of my patients used to say, they can leave the hospital and go back home without feeling like a stranger within their own family.

I do not mean to say that patients who have been hospitalized at our facilities and go out to work or study are no longer "delirious" or "hearing voices." However, that does not prevent them from leading a professional life and meeting new people. Our focus on more "patho-

---

6 The Margaridas Hostel worked as a half-way house and, I believe, their treatment was unprecedented in Brazil. This treatment was ac-cepted by an insurance group, but later rejected due to bureaucratic issues with the National Institute of Medical Care and Social Security / National Institute of Social Security (INAMPS / INPS). The facilities are still in operation, but they only receive private patients at the "Mar-garidas" Psychotherapy Emergency.

logical" events is different from most of the other facilities I knew.

I do not believe that my patients feel any reservations in telling me what they feel, think, rant, and rave in delusion. I believe that, thanks to everything I have lived and am living, I am able to establish a friendly connection between them and me. It is equivalent to the connection that exists between patients, when they tell each other the way they feel while keeping the therapeutic staff on the sidelines, as we can see in most hospitals.

The difficulty that therapists have to put themselves in a patient's place comes as a result of a lack of adequate treatment for their own pathological narcissism, of which therapists necessarily must rid themselves upon entering the office, so that they can reach directly into the core issue of a patient's problem.

What happens is that therapists fail to go deeper into the primitive stages that are absolutely necessary to the emotional development of the Other. Otherwise, they assume a neutral position and remain silent, as if patients were always highly uninteresting as far as the material they are bringing forth. Moreover, therapists may make good or bad interpretations, according to their own health. If they are unwell, they will make self-references as a way of transference.

As I had already mentioned in another book, it is extremely difficult for transferences to happen, but when they do take place, therapists rarely recognize them. They mistake projective identifications with transference, placing themselves in the center of the patient's world. Or, worse, patients in general do not react to it. I would like to mention, for example, the case of a patient who had been depressed for five years, and to whom the therapist said on the third session that he, the patient, wanted to kill himself because he was angry at the therapist.

It is incredible how intelligent patients usually "agree" with such absurdities. Well, if someone is only getting to know me, but has been thinking about killing himself for the past five years, his history of suicide is not related to me. It could be related to something outside of him (an external factor), but it mainly concerns the patient's internal "struggles." Would the patient's agreement with the careless therapist have happened due to pure disregard? I do not know.[7] All I know is that I would not listen to that without reacting properly. It is like taking material from oral to Oedipal content. The thing is that the silent patient creates a false self and feels satisfied, but a "hole" remains in his personality and it is not filled by the treatment.

My militancy in the Brazilian Communist Party was very important to my personal life and, especially, to my professional background, due to the knowledge and practice I acquired then. Without knowledge about Engels, Lenin, and Marx—notwithstanding how rudimen-

---

7 In a study group with Maria Antonia Rocha e Silva, Rosa Maria Saraiva, and Agenor Alvarenga, I was able to understand why patients don't rebel when they hear such stupidity. And I completely agree with the explanation I was given. These patients are so pathologically narcissistic that they can't admit it to themselves the remote idea that they have selected an incompetent therapist. The incompetent analyst joins in the patient's self-destructive impulses, since their interpretation does not reach the suicidal motivation.

tary this knowledge may be—one can hardly understand the thesis and antithesis of affections, thoughts, and conducts. One would hardly understand Freud.

At a certain point throughout my path as a psychoanalyst, I was able to take part in some a great work at "Pensão Protegida" (Protected Hostel), recommended by Social Psychiatrist and Professor Luiz da Rocha Cerqueira since 1969. Individuals who no longer needed any hospital treatment could remain there as guests, receiving a better (more adequate) service than that of a hotel, since there was a supporting psychiatric infrastructure with psychiatrists and psychologists. Each individual paid as much as they could afford, and that is why the facilities were able to support themselves and become a role model for many others founded later in Brazil. "Pensão Protegida" was the subject of one of my presentations at a congress in Cuba in 1986. It was titled "Mental Health in a Neo-Capitalist Country: Brazil" and inspired the admiration of members of the audience. Likewise, the way "Pensão Protegida" worked is described in my 1981 book *Personalidade Psicótica e Psicose* [Psychotic Personality and Psycosis.]

Something else that is very important to the development of all the work I perform is the fact that I worked at several pioneering care centers. I started out at the Pinel Clinic in Porto Alegre in 1960, where in addition to the contact with my patients I also enjoyed my downtime in the middle of the night shift to read everything I could get my hands on, from Socrates to Dostoyevsky to Graciliano Ramos. My contact with Marcelo Blaya, who introduced Psychoanalysis to the hospital, was very enlightening to me.

In Rio de Janeiro, I took part in the pioneering work of Professor I. de L. Neves Manta, who created outpatient facilities for the ill at IPASE (Institute for Social Security and Assistance to State Servants,) where I had the privilege to work with Professor Cerqueira. Concomitantly, I was part of the pioneering work being done at the first Day Hospital within the INSS (Social Security National Institute) network in 1968, located at the Medical Treatment Pavillion at Avenida Marechal Rondon, where I worked with occupational therapy, psychotherapy and physical therapy with selected social and psychological services. It did not work... because it did work. It faded from everybody's memory, except for those involved in it.[8]

Later came the first Dynamic Clinic at Vila Pinheiros, a private institution where I worked as the Chief of Clinic with great psychoanalysts, such as General Supervisor Walderedo Ismael de Oliveira. There, psychoanalytical groups started to work with psychotic patients, coordinated by psychoanalysts Ismael de Oliveira, Paulo Marchou and Maria Luiza Pinto—believe it or not, they helped some patients in very severe stages. For the so-called neurotics, I believe these groups worked better than those outside the hospital. However, when these groups were extinct, psychotic patients were referred to individual therapy sessions, which represented true failure to them.

---

8 Things that work in Brazil are often destroyed because they go against the establishment.

Today, I still have the privilege to continue to follow up on a great majority of these patients, because I have been treating some with analytical-based psychotherapy and am interested in them and try to learn how their life is going. As I have already written about in my book *Psicoterapia do Paciente Psicótico*[9] [Psychotherapy of Psychotic Patients,] most of those who were referred to individual therapy have abandoned treatment and are now chronic cases. Some have continued their individual therapy, but were unable to overcome reacutization. Others have committed suicide. The ones who were referred to psychotherapy were able to be cured and live well.

For what I learned about using psychoanalysis in direct contact with psychotic patients during my 34 years of observation of psychotic patients in therapy sessions, I am now convinced that Freud was right when he said that psychotic patients are not eligible for therapy. That is why for so many years I have been recommending a specific psychotherapeutic model for psychotic patients that would be based on a psychoanalytical foundation, but with techniques adequate to the case, as I have already been doing. This subject was developed in *Psicoterapia do Paciente Psicótico*.

I will start up this book about filicide from my point of view on the Oedipus Myth, a subject I have studied and previously published in *Psicoterapia do Paciente Psicótico*. The study is titled "Oedipus at the Crossroads" and it exposes the subject more clearly.

---

9 The book was originally published in 1982 and reedited by KBR. DAMETTO, Carmem. *Psicoterapia do Paciente Psicótico*. Petrópolis: KBR, 2012.

Here is a warning: Both the subject and the explanations and examples may seem repetitive. It is so because this issue is very hard to understand, so I try to make myself clear in several ways.

Oedipus at the Crossroads[10]

Whenever I think about the Oedipus Complex, the first thing that comes to mind is the love triangle formed by father, mother, and son/daughter in a position that Melanie Klein calls "depressive" in the emotional development of babies. "Depressive position" and "Oedipal phase" are synonyms and those who are able to resolve them adequately achieve emotional growth. However, we must emphasize that individuals have such ability from birth.

I will explain myself better: I continue to think that many people have not even started to reach what we call "Oedipus Complex" in psychoanalysis. For them, emotional maturity was blocked well before such stage, at a more primitive level, in the paranoid schizophrenia phase. Others were incapable of reaching paranoid schizophrenia and remained in an autoerotic position. They were unable to take the "qualitative" leap referred to

---

10 In: DAMETTO, Carmem. *Psicoterapia do Paciente Psicótico, op. cit.* This work was prepared for presentation at the International Psychotherapy Congress, which took place August 1982 in Rio de Janeiro. We couldn't go through with the presentation for reasons that are unknown to me. The subject was slightly adapted for the book.

by Freud, which consists of a resolution of emotions at a mental level by using autoerotic narcissism and the consequent formation of ego. Ego is then formed from a new force, narcissism, which according to Freud is added to autoeroticism and makes babies resolve their problems at a mental level. It does not stop being autoerotic until they can do it at the pathological or healthy level.

Narcissism is then the qualitative leap in life instinct, which goes from the body to the mind and is possibly driven by the force of autoerotic libido. Regular people were able to take this qualitative leap and developed well. According to Klein, there are children who stop their development in the first mental position, paranoid schizophrenia. Other babies are able to take the qualitative leap in most part of their libido and become psychosomatically ill. They are unable to have hallucinations or delusions, so they attack their body directly, just as schizophrenic patients attack their minds to undo their ego. A patient, for example, had ulcerative colitis by attacking his intestines. Both types of patients may commit suicide or die after these internal attacks due to an unresolved case of autoerotic narcissism.

Drug addict, hypochondriac patients have the same mechanisms of psychosomatic patients. Their libido remains mostly autoerotic. That is why they are so difficult to treat, even though their personality in great part remains "normal." Maybe this is my way of explaining the creation of ego. It is just that, while working at a hospital with patients who were pure and simple autoerotic instinct, I was able to observe the level of fragmentation that some of them had achieved. I could go as far as saying that there were no remains of ego left. They are the so-called schizophrenic patients, but they will actually only become schizophrenic once they get a little better.

Being schizophrenic implies having an ego, which is formed by internal autoerotic urges when an individual faces reality. Sometimes, even the unconscious mind of the patient has been partially destroyed and needs to be reformed. As a matter of fact, narcissism is autoerotic, since the patient is all urge and autoeroticism. I'd like to make it clear that—whether it is right or wrong from a theoretical standpoint—I believe that all affectionate manifestations are autoerotic if the patient is for or against himself and/or others during this primitive stage I've been talking about.

In regards to the ego, its formation and disassembling, I mainly refer to people with a psychotic personality[11] who suffer from a psychotic disorder of any nature. Actually, upon observing someone who is psychotically ill, one thing that has caught our attention is that the father is not present, not even in the clinical history. During a properly-performed anamnesis, the father only appears as a significant figure in the medical history of neurotic

---

11 According to Bion, in "Differentiation of the Psychotic from the Non-Psychotic Personalities," a section of his book entitled "Second Thoughts," a psychotic personality is established with the massive use of projective identifications. It doesn't mean that an individual with a psychotic personality is ill. Projective identifications that may, at a later time, become delusional ideas, references, hallucinations, and aggressive conduct can only exist in the presence of ego, notwithstanding how rudimentary it may be. Bion also says that another characteristic is the absence of repression as a defense mechanism.

and/or psychotic patients who are extremely ill, when fathers have taken on the role of mothers in their absence or absolute incapacity. However, it bears repeating that the father in this case is not a father, but a "mother," or maybe even neither; for neurotic patients, fathers have always played the role of fathers. Those who are neurotically ill or have a neurotic personality and reach the Oedipus Complex are able to resolve it, thus becoming healthy individuals; otherwise, if they don't overcome it, they manifest a neurotic illness.

"Oedipal fantasies"[12] in psychotic patients only exist in appearance. Schizophrenics commonly say that they want to have sexual relations with their mothers. Nevertheless, in this case, it's not about their father's wife, but a woman who is divested from the "role" of mother to the son and wife to the father.

I'd like to make a side note and mention an example of how I handle this type of "fantasy."

***

Clinical Session: transference as resistance

A few years ago, a patient had the following dia-

---

12 Actually, they are not fantasies, but the verbalization of incest feelings that are alive, painful, or pleasant. Oedipal fantasies are present in normal or neurotic individuals. Psychotic individuals live it concretely; therefore, it is not a fantasy.

log with me:

> Patient: I had a dream with you last night.
>
> Me: Really? And...
>
> P: I was "having" you in my dream.
>
> Me: Do you expect me to waste our upcoming months trying to understand your Oedipal fantasies?
>
> P: I think the material is important.
>
> Me: So do I, but I think your problem has been resolved. Congratulations. And congratulations for having such good taste, because I'm a cougar. Did your father kill you in your dream?
>
> P: No [laughter]. That is why I like being treated by you, instead of wasting my time—as I have wasted these past thirteen years.
>
> Me: So your problem is resolved. How about we discuss the work you're about to start doing tomorrow?
>
> P: Yeah, I'm really frightened about it.

We went on with our session to treat the narcissistic problem from which the patient is trying to "escape." He is a schizophrenic in full recovery, an engineer, and he is trying to find a job to return to the normal life that remained on hold for a few years, during which he was going through a psychoanalytical treatment that "helped" him become intellectualized and more psychotic. I didn't work with the transference material, because this patient was resorting to transference as a means to resist the true acknowledgement of the narcissistic issues that did not allow him to lead a normal life.

Actually, transference moments in non-intellectualized psychotic patients are extremely rare, which makes me wonder more and more each time whether it is worth it to waste our valuable time—both the patient's and mine—discussing the matter. Patients need help to resolve severe cases, such as false self, narcissism, filicide, and suicide, which naturally encompass the resolution of Oedipal problems as well as others that exist at a psychotic level. The fact that this patient in particular told me that he had dreamt of having sexual relations with me, without any retaliation from his father, meant that he was using repression as a defense mechanism—something that hadn't happened before—and as we discussed his narcissistic, filicidal, and suicidal problems, his psychotic symptoms were being resolved one by one until he arrived at the depressive or Oedipal stage.

A sample of how repression is used for defensive purposes is the dream itself. Now, what the patient needs is to do is face life and look for a job, even if it's something far from his imagined narcissistic proportions (he'll try to be a salesperson.)

And why did I say I was a "cougar"? To give the patient some peace of mind, in that he can have any fantasies he wants with me without judging that I'll feel seduced by it or try to seduce him.

It's important to mention that the way that I talk is spontaneous, "automatic," a result of my own life experiences, which went from being disorders to something that was overcome and elaborated. However, they come to life as in a conversation with a friend. I don't believe this should be imitated by people who haven't had their basic problems resolved, such as pathological narcissism and suicide (filicide).

***

In neurotic patients, incest takes place at the fantasy level. In turn, with psychotic patients it does happen in reality, in a psychotic rupture seen in both son and mother. The Oedipus Myth transcribed below may be interpreted differently if we consider it under the light of what we know about psychosis.

"Upon the death of his father Labdacus while he was still in his teenage years, Laius fled to Eleian Pisa in fear of being killed by the two men who had invaded his kingdom. There, King Pelops welcomed him. The King had a son, Chrysippus, who fell in love with Laius when he first laid eyes on him—the feeling was mutual. They surrendered to their love, but the secret was exposed and reached Pelops, who was deeply ashamed and did not know how to hide his abashment. Afraid of his father's reaction, Chrysippus killed himself. Laius ran away from the kingdom. Pelops cursed him and Fate took care of fulfilling the prophecy: Laius shall be killed by his son, who will then marry his own mother.

Laius returned to Thebes, his kingdom, and was successful in having his throne usurped for him. Little by little, he forgot his love for Chrysippus and his regrets. He married Jocasta, who one day announced she was expecting a child. Laius was saddened and felt persecuted due to his remorse and Pelops' curse. He consulted Apollo's oracle at Delphi, which confirmed the curse: His son would indeed kill him and marry his own mother."

Effectively, as we know from the tragedy, Laius ordered to have Oedipus killed after birth, but we also know that it did not happen because of shepherd's intervention.[13]

"Upon learning of the curse, Oedipus left his home in Corinth, where they had welcomed him, and went towards his former "unknown" kingdom. On a crossroads, he killed a stranger. That was his father.

Later he deciphered the riddle of the Sphinx and saved Thebes from a curse, thus acquiring the right to marry Jocasta, the queen, a widow whose king had been killed at a crossroads by a stranger (Oedipus).

Oedipus became aware that he did kill his own father and married his own mother, with whom he had four children. The prophecy had been fulfilled. Upon realizing it, Jocasta killed herself and Oedipus blinded himself with a piercing object.

From his four children, Antigone was the one who remained by her father's side until his death. Ismene replaced her father and ruled the kingdom. His two sons had been abandoned by their father and killed each other. Covered by a shroud, Oedipus died when

---

13 Oedipus was taken by the shepherd to another kingdom, where he was raised by the king. While growing up, he heard from someone about the prophecy of his criminal future and, since he didn't want to kill his father or have relations with his mother—who he believed were the king and queen raising him—he went to another kingdom, more precisely Thebes, where his biological parents lived.

the depths of Earth busted open to receive him."

Only Freud, the genius, was able to connect Oedi-pus' tragedy to the resolution of neurotic problems, since fundamentally it oozes psychosis: Homosexuality[14], par-ricide, suicide, filicide, fratricide, and incest. Filicide is concrete; therefore, it does not represent a fantasy in neu-rosis, but a real event. At birth, Oedipus was condemned by his father to die, since the father gave the child away to a peasant so that he could be killed—the father was prob-ably running away from a possible homosexual and nar-cissistic pathological connection[15] with his son.

Parricide becomes secondary. It takes place later, but also concretely. However, the father no longer plays the "role" of a father, but that of a stranger at a crossroads. As it happens with psychotic patients, their parents are strangers to him at certain times in their lives. Jocasta is no longer a mother figure either. She is an attractive wom-an to whom Oedipus has the right to marry. And so he does, in reality, not in fantasy. Neither of them play their roles of mother and son, respectively, and become two hu-mans without a common past in the psychotic experience of this tragedy. It is when they become "aware" of it, and see the affective bonds they once share, that they return to their respective roles—the psychosis is "cured." Jocasta then commits suicide upon this awareness, another psy-chotic act. Oedipus stabs himself in the eye and is pun-

14 Despite the fact that homosexuality is no longer included in the list of mental illnesses, it is hard to make homosexuals believe it and stop to suffer and seek treatment. Decrees do not cure suffering.

15 Because he was afraid of being killed by him, as the curse said.

ished until the earth swallows him up. Basically, the entire tragedy is a psychotic situation that, when unfolded, shows the different aspects that neurotic patients would resolve in fantasy and psychosis due to a lack of symbolic bond, but are concretely shown here in physical acts. The main problem related to this tragedy is the creation of a pathologically narcissistic couple.

Why do I consider them a pathologically narcissistic couple?

In *Personalidade Psicótica e Psicose*, I wrote about the creation of a pathologically narcissistic couple when individuals fall in love with themselves in another person. This is what happens to people who, despite the appearance of each being half of a couple, are actually married to themselves in the other person.

I believe this is what Freud alluded to when he demanded that his patients practiced "sexual abstinence." The way I see it, someone who is going through treatment, even for something not so severe, shouldn't be making a serious commitment to someone else, such as getting married or moving in together. That would be creating a couple that is not functioning at the genital level—or, as M. Klein would say, that has reached a depressive position. Throughout my years of practice, I have had the displeasure of witnessing two cases in which patients were unable to listen to me and wound up leaving their lives unresolved. One got married and then separated a few years later, with three small children, due to little arguments. The other one, a psychotic patient, also insisted in getting married. The family was warned about the risk that he would be exposing himself to, but accepted the fact. The patient had a psychotic crisis right after the wedding, then another one with the birth of his first child, which could have been avoided had he followed my advice. Considering the family's attitude, I gave up treating that patient. The immediate family (father and mother) thought they could just "pass the problem along" by marrying him off.

Escaping from treatment through sexual or pseudosexual acts is very common. It's one date here, another one there... I think this is something that no mortals, healthy or ill, can avoid. But I take care to avoid separations or couplings, whichever their nature, during treatment—unless the person was already about to get married or separated when they first started treatment. I've always said that people who don't meet the minimum requirements to get married do so anyway, sometimes to escape their families, sometimes to escape themselves. In other words, they're trying to avoid facing their own loneliness. The "other half" everybody says they have found is just a fallacy. If someone is "one half," they cannot get married. It is my understanding that someone should only get married if, in and of themselves, they already carried their "two halves" within. Maybe, then, these people wouldn't want to get married or would find different ways to have a relationship with the opposite sex.

I would like to recall what I wrote in another book: Oftentimes, teenagers get married so they don't get hospitalized. The girlfriend, who is herself close to a breakdown, becomes his hospital and nurse. The marriage doesn't last long, because it only serves the purpose of escaping madness and does not help fulfill adulthood in what one can give the other in terms of affection. The biggest problem is that, in general, there are many children left for grandmothers to take care of, that is, when they don't end up with one of the parents, who'll raise them surrounded by hate because these children represent a union that is no longer desired.

I call this kind of "marriage" between young people a "covert psychiatric internment." It is socially acceptable and performed with the purpose of preventing the explicit manifestation of madness. Apparently, young people are "in love," when in fact they are narcissistically intertwined (psychotically) in a sturdy net of projective identification. Therefore, one cannot live without the other. Overall, such "intertwining" comes undone as soon as the woman gets pregnant and then separation comes quickly. When a child is born, the pseudobond is broken.

This is a common fact, even though some "couples" remain together for many, many years, especially if a child becomes sick (psychotic) and sheds some light on their sick relationship. After all, husband and wife will have something in common: Someone to take care of, or a reason to fight. The child will become their Christ, who comes to save their marriage, trying to remain sick for the longest time possible.

Narcissistic behavior is also evident in the Oedipus tragedy, both due to the history of all protagonists and the actions they performed. Laius has a psychotic crisis when he learns that he will have a child. When Jocasta married Oedipus, she knew very well, albeit unconsciously, that he was her son. Likewise, he knew she was his mother. Therefore, they made a connection that is only possible within psychotic or pathological narcissism. It's as if they would say: "We are superior beings; we can face this kind of relationship that nobody else can withstand." And they too, upon becoming aware of their own knowledge and realizing they were living in psychosis (the role of the mother and the role of the son had been undone) had no other way out but death.

That is the same ending we see in the myth of Narcissus, in which he commits suicide upon recognizing himself.

Why can't Narcissus take the pain inside and has to commit suicide?

a. Because he can't fulfill his own ideals, especially that of greatness, that he had of himself.

b. Because his filicidal parents had infused in him the idea that he had to die.

c. Because he can't "see himself" alone, without the help of someone from the outside—a therapist, I should say.

d. Because he failed to internalize a complete object. When he does achieve it, maybe for a split second, he kills himself because he then sees his parents, who expect suicide to take place.

We could also add that the same happened to

Adam and Eve: When they became aware *one* of *the other* as a *complete object*, they were punished by God, the Superego, with the loss of their immortality. God committed filicide and the fact must be included in other myths of humanity. Actually, Adam and Eve knew they could not challenge divine orders under the penalty of death. But so they did, when they knew each other and got killed at the immortality level. For pathologically narcissists, getting to know themselves is extremely threatening, since their ego is fragile. It is the ego of a psychotic, whose castrating superego is also filicidal; it is the voice of their parents as destructive partial objects, and the voice of their own self-destructing being. Danger is in the possibility of suicide.

Narcissism

Sampa [São Paulo] [16]
Caetano Veloso

Something happens to my heart
Where Ipiranga and Avenida São João meet.
When I first arrived here, I didn't understand
The harsh concrete poetry of your street corners,
The discrete lack of elegance of your girls.

I was yet to meet Rita Lee,
Your most complete personification.
Something happens to my heart
Where Ipiranga and Avenida São João meet.

When I first faced you, I did not see my own face.
I called poor taste what I saw—poor taste, poor
taste.
Narcissus sees ugliness in whatever is not a mirror.
The mind unravels at what is not really old.

---

16 Partial lyrics of Caetano Veloso's "Sampa," which geniously shows a case of pathological narcissism.

Unlike the time before we became mutants.

The beginning was hard.
I rejected what was unfamiliar to me.
Those who come from a happy dream of a city
Quickly learn how to call you reality.
Because you're the opposite of the opposite
Of the opposite of the opposite...

This book begins with the myth of Narcissus, from his birth until his death—rather, from his conception to his death. I will comment on that I believe to be relevant to clinical observations of psychotic patients and their families or group of relatives. Here is a partial transcription quoted from *Mitologia*, volume 11, published by Editora Abril Cultural.

> "In the lands of Boeotia ran the waters of Cephissus, the God and the river. Nymphs could not walk safely by the riverbanks, because as soon as Cephissus saw them, he would try to trap them in his torrents. And so it happened to a nymph by the name of Liriope. She was strolling by the river on a summer day when the water came up, surrounded her and took her in sudden passion. For months, Liriope carried the fruit of that undesired love inside herself. Her life, which had been peaceful until then, became filled with sadness and tiredness, with woes that could only be whispered through the dark shadows of the forest."

Regarding the formation of a psychotic or pathologically narcissistic family, I must warn you that, first of all, narcissism is inherent to all human beings. However, at a pathological level, it is manifested as a frank or masked psychosis; nevertheless, it is always a psychosis that is ready to be passed along to a relative and, if it is latent, it may hatch into a psychotic episode. I usually state that wherever we identify a psychotic patient—narcissistic, according to Freud—there is an entire family group that functions in the same psychotic way.

I insist on the formation of a pathologically narcissistic couple. Narcissus parents reaffirm what I mentioned about my clinical experience: Only an extremely pathologically narcissistic couple could have a psychotic son. In this myth, the river (father) fulfilled his needs, achieved his goal and realized a desire that is well-known to everyone: Having a nymph. He did not worry about her desires or bothered about what others might think of him. He was only concerned with himself.

And that is how a pathologically narcissistic (psychotic) patient thinks and acts. *For him, the other and the world outside do not exist.* There is only himself, his desires, and his frustrations. Narcissus' mother, Liriope the Nymph, obviously knew about the horrible reputation of the river. However, she did not listen to the facts of reality. The promises that the river made to her were the same that he had made to other nymphs, but they knew how to escape his deception. She, Liriope, did not escape him, though. It was not only the "betrayal" of the river, but above all her own denial, her haughtiness—her own pathological narcissism, after all. She only listened to her own voice, which convinced herself that nothing would happen to HER, maybe because she believed to be so superior to the river.[17]

They were equivalent, both the river and the nymph, each one of them living in isolation with their own emotions. They were lonely, as any pathologically narcissistic patient, a psychotic individual, or someone with a psychotic personality. The myth continues to confirm the theory that I have been developing, for the father (river) lost interest in his son, which was expected. The mother, however, did not.

> "Nevertheless, when the son was born, Liriope's face lit up again with extreme joy. The boy, who was named Narcissus, was handsome and gracious. As a grown up, he would certainly be loved by goddesses, nymphs, and mortal women alike."

Liriope got revenge for her suffering and had a son that would make her shine, since he will be coveted by all women. She was "well resolved." Other women will love him. However, as any good old pathologically narcissistic individual, the presence of the Other in general is uncomfortable.

Narcissus became a threat to her and, consequently, she must know whether her son will live long. Well, no woman who truly wants to have a baby is concerned with knowing how much longer the child will live.[18] Be-

---

17 Please refer to Tolstoy's *The Death of Ivan Ilyich*.

18 Actually, the woman is more worried about knowing whether the baby is perfect, that is, if she has all her fingers and toes. In other words, she wants to know about the baby as an individual being, not as a strange and uncomfortable presence.

ing concerned about death, sure, because it is right there for everybody, but she experiences an ambivalent effect as well. Her concern with the exact date of his death is very strange. It has something to do with pathological filicide, which is very common in pathologically narcissistic couples.

> "Anxious to know if Narcissus would live for many years, the young nymph went to Tiresias, a blind prophet whose fame had then started to move beyond the Boeotia borders. 'Yes, he will have a long life,' the blind prophet answered. 'As long as he never knows himself.'"

According to the myth, the great risk of suicide for psychotic patients lies in when they start to be "introduced" to themselves during treatment. As they get to know themselves, they start to notice that they are not as wonderful as the image they had painted of themselves. First of all, they learn that there are others and, secondly, that other individuals may have new and good things to bring. This makes patients who had been in an almost completely paranoid schizophrenic state to move, [19]little by little, towards a depressive position. That is why we often have to hospitalize patients for a few days when everybody can clearly see that they've made a turn for the better. Even therapists can notice a rough sketch of object images being internalized and the beginning of integration.

Patients are the only ones who cannot perceive

---

19 Or earlier, autoerotic.

and feel the process. They actually feel bad and want to commit suicide. For them, it is so painful to know themselves as it was for Narcissus, who gave in to the seductive idea of suicide when he saw his own reflection in the water. Actually, if they had continuous insights and cured themselves all of a sudden, psychotic patients would commit suicide. They would not be able to quickly metabolize the enormous amount of new information provided by their id; they would be frightened and feel impotent before such task. That is why you have to be very careful when treating psychotic patients, so that they don't die from the cure.[20]

And, I would like to make it very clear that the suicide of psychotics has nothing to do with anyone. With their death, they do not pay tribute to anyone, nor do they seek revenge against anyone. Psychotic individuals suffer too much when they get to know themselves and, if the only way to avoid such pain is suicide, they will take advantage of a moment of desperation. The purpose of these considerations is to warn certain psychoanalysts who still think that the suicide of psychotic individuals is dedicated to internal figures—which the patient doesn't have—or to the analyst. If that were the case, under both circumstances psychotic individuals would not commit suicide because they would have internalized object images or established some sort of relationship of love or hate with their analyst, who represents the outside world.

I believe many therapists project their own inter-

---

20 This was the case with Jocasta. Upon having an enormous insight, she committed suicide.

ests and connections towards the patient, who will only actually become aware that the therapist exists as a person well into the treatment. Going back to the myth, we can verify this fact when Echo, a nymph, falls in love with Narcissus and he does not become aware of her love. I will comment on the deep and diversified meaning of the myth throughout this book, because I have noticed that many psychoanalysts either ignore myths because they are disinterested in the human truths that they represent, or do not apply their correct interpretation in clinical practice. Having a solid and wide cultural basis beyond psychoanalytical knowledge is not a recommendation for professionals; it is a requirement. Didn't Freud resort to mythology to illustrate his doctrine?

> "(...) Narcissus, as an adult, stumbled upon his own image reflected in the undisturbed surface of a fountain. He fell in love so madly with what he saw that he spent days there, looking at himself while being consumed by hunger, thirst, and solitude."

It is clear. By killing himself slowly, Narcissus was only thinking of himself and nobody else.

There are other versions of the myth. In one of them, Narcissus would have drowned, but the important thing is that he ended up dying when he wanted to effectively know himself. He ignores the outside world that, in the myth, is represented by Echo. At the clinic, such role is personified by therapists. Within the family, they are parents or siblings. In society, by the individuals who are part of it, with their social rules to which psychotic patients have a hard time adjusting, not because they are absurd—and they often are—but because they turn a "deaf ear" and, at the same time, a "blind eye" to life. They only see themselves; they feel, hear, smell themselves. They completely ignore the rest, the Others. In regards to Echo...

> "As soon as he became aware that the young nymph was looking at him, Narcissus ran away. He did not want anybody's love. Echo went after him. She got closer to her loved one several times and she lacked no words to express her affection."

Once again, I stress the formation of a pathologically narcissistic couple. Had Echo not lived in her own world, like Liriope, she would have given up loving Narcissus when she was first rejected. Apparently, she and Narcissus had the opposite conduct of his parents, but we know that, dialectically, the opposites are the same. However, Echo is not heard by Narcissus, nor does she notice that he does not want her. They all live in their private worlds and are not concerned with the Other. The Other doesn't exist.

Going back to the myth:

> "One day, Narcissus distanced himself from his fellow hunters and, while trying to find them, he shouted, 'Is there anybody there?' In the middle of the forest, the question was asked back to him. The answer came from Echo, who pointlessly tried to tell him that there was somebody there; she was that somebody and she had so much love to give and could make him happy. Caught by surprise, Narcissus looked around,

but saw nobody. Then he shouted again, 'Come!' The same voice repeated his plead. The young man looked through the bushes, trees and flowers, he ran left and right and, in total despair, he said, 'Are you running away from me?' From the forest, Echo answered, 'Are you running away from me?'"

And so is the behavior of psychotic patients before the love that is offered to them by a therapist or any family member. Many therapists insist in ignoring such fact and think it better to believe that the patient is listening to their words. Echo speaks to herself. Narcissus only hears what he can. It is no use for us, therapists, to keep ignoring this basic clinical fact, which has already been pointed out by Freud in his *On Narcissism: An Introduction*. In addition to the words they'll only hear when they are able to, psychotic patients require a behavior consistent with these words. Psychoanalytical interpretations only make them get worse.[21] Beyond words, they need care. Therapists have to be their Echo nymph, but only after their own pathological narcissism is overcome; in other words, they need to repeat a million times things that psychotic patients need to hear and feel in order to get cured.

Within the forest, Echo and Narcissus behave as patients in a psychiatric hospital who are communicating for a few seconds—for example, when they ask for a cigarette—only to immediately isolate themselves, each in their own world. This kind of behavior is frequently seen

---

21 According to Bion, in his book *Volviendo a Pensar*, psychoanalysis on psychotic patients only serves the purpose of making them chronic.

in an operative group,[22] clearly revealing the deep solitude of psychotics. Only a patient who is in a better place can approach another patient to offer support, or even to contradict him, thus creating dialog and more communication. Overall, each patient only speaks to the group coordinator. Even in psychotic psychoanalysis, there is no dialog. They, patient and therapist, will always be Echo and Narcissus in parallel conversations, without ever crossing ways, turning what could be a good relationship into something sterilized, as it happened with Echo in the myth.

In a last attempt to find his friends, Narcissus called them again:

> "'Let's reunite!' Echo thought that the invitation was to her. She ran to his direction and tried to give him a sweet embrace. Narcissus let go of her anxious hands, jumped up to his feet and disappeared into the dark forest. Ashamed and desperate, the nymph hid amid the vegetation, covering her eyes with the leaves to camouflage her tears. Pain and suffering took a hold of her fragile body. She thinned down each day. She got wrinkled. She got sadder. Her eyes became stones and she turned into a bedrock. Only the voice of others, reflected in her invisible and unfortunate throat, still reverberated throughout the universe."

And that was the end of pathologically narcissistic Echo. Just as her, the mentally ill only become chronic. They lose their feelings, they become blunt, and they turn

---

22 Operative groups are described in my book *O Psicótico e seu tratamento*, *Op. Cit.*

into stone.

"As Echo, other nymphs from the waters and the forests tried in vain to win Narcissus' love. In disbelief about the indifference of the handsome young man, one of them raised her hands to the sky to ask the immortals for assistance. That was when she put a terrible curse on Liriope's son: May he love me one day and never have the object of his affection. Nemesis, the goddess of vengeance, heard her plead and answered it, guiding Narcissus' steps towards the fountain where he would find his fatal destiny.

Exhausted from running away from the nymph that had been after him, the young man bent over the water to quench his thirst and then clearly saw his reflection in the crystal clear waters. His handsome face won his heart. Enchanted, Narcissus smiled at the image and then got the same smile in return. He waved and the reflection in the water waved back.

Believing that he had been corresponded in that sudden infatuation, the young man reached out to touch that darling face. The image in the mirror was gone with the ripples; it escaped him the same way he had escaped the advances of the nymphs. Handsome Narcissus was then aware of how much a non-corresponded love hurts. His suffering hovered over the clear surface of the fountain. Bitter tears came down his eyes. His voice was faltering when he cursed the one who had once put a curse on him."

That was when Narcissus' sudden cure was first sketched and he no longer went looking for his friends through the forest. He then realized the reality that surrounded him and gave in to despair.

"His disturbed thoughts brought the sweet image of Echo to mind; she, who always answered to his voice, without showing him in any other way that she was able to hear him. Now Narcissus knew the deep pain of loneliness. Near the fountain, unable to walk away from his own reflection, Liriope's son stopped eating, forgot about quenching his own thirst, and could no longer rest. Little by little, he withered away until he collapsed, lifeless, on the field. 'Goodbye, my darling, my love in vain,' were his last words."

And that was how Narcissus committed suicide— as psychotic, pathologically narcissistic patients who kill themselves for being in disagreement with themselves, not with Others; that would be the case of psychotic patients with internalized object images, who would try to or be successful in committing suicide while paying tribute to said images, as Freud said, thus constituting more of a homicide attempt than a true suicide. It was not in vain that Freud said that "a narcissistic individual is the object of himself" and, in order to treat him, he contraindicated the process he had created himself for neurotic patients.

In addition to Narcissus' suicidal ideations, the myth sheds a light on the unconscious filicidal and pathological wishes of his parents. Upon contemplating himself on the fountain as a total object, Narcissus saw his parents as total objects. He then realized that his death wish was an extension of his parents' unconscious desire, and that maybe he really was *indeed just a manifestation of the filicidal wish of his parents.* He realized he was *nobody.* That was when his suicide became a reality, because—Narcissus felt completely alone. There was nobody by his side, or even inside himself, with sufficient love to keep him alive.

Such is the case of psychotic patients. The better they get and the more they feel like a person, with introjected total objects, the higher the risk of their committing suicide because they begin to notice the filicidal, pathological wishes of their parents and, consequently, their own suicidal wishes.

That is why I'd like to emphasize that we need to pay close attention to patients who are showing some improvement. There are many intense depressing moments at each insight, with a larger perception of themselves and others. Sometimes it is even convenient to hospitalize patients. I know it is hard for families, therapists and, above all, patients to understand that precisely because they are getting better, there is a greater risk and they need more intense care. We commonly hear statements such as, "How did he commit suicide now that he was doing so well at work and at home?" It was because, upon knowing himself, knowing his total objects, he realized he was completely alone. Not even the therapist understood him. In general, therapists convince themselves that these patients had "an accident."

One thing that calls our attention is that Narcissus dies in the water (his father);[23] that is, he reaches an Oedipal phase. At a clinic, it is common to have psychotic patients experience extreme difficulty to improve, because they are frightened about being killed by their fathers. It is not overreacting.

---

23 It really shows the repetition when Laius ordered Oedipus' death.

Fathers have a harder time than mothers to allow sons to get better. They don't have major issues with their daughters, but sons make fathers uncomfortable. To quote what the father of one of my patients once said, it's "as if there is no room for two men in my house."

Another male patient once mentioned that his father "wanted all his women," which is a case of a primitive horde, when men competed for a single place in the world. On the other hand, upon getting better many male patients also "order" an illness or the death of their fathers.

In families that are less mixed in by projective identifications, there is a possibility that one or several individuals have a disorder. However, there is no need for anyone to die.

Overlapping the Myth of Narcissus and the Tragedy of Oedipus

Narcissus vs. Oedipus
Filicide – Suicide

1 - Laius vs. Jocasta — Oedipus

Laius and Jocasta represent pathological narcissism and filicide; they are able to keep a connection with the outside world. They order their son Oedipus to be killed; he, who was already born pathologically narcissistic, suffers a filicide attempt. Oedipus grows up denying everything he already knew unconsciously and, throughout the tragedy, he reveals his psychotic, parricide, incestuous, suicidal and pathologically filicidal behavior—much like his parents—, for his two sons wound up killing each other. He too commits suicide after having an insight about himself through the revelations of blind Tiresias (outside world, superego). However, before killing himself, he is able to establish an affective bond with objects outside himself—much like his parents did.

As people, Laius and Jocasta are "whole" figures who are almost completely separate and can make affective exchanges despite their mutual moments of invasion. We know that Laius was a psychotic individual, for he had had a homosexual romance with a male friend. Consequently, Jocasta must have been a very disturbed individual if she was united with him. Their marriage could make the list of what I call pathologically narcissistic marriages.

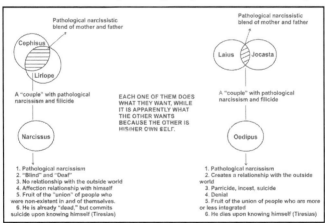

2 - Liriope vs. Cephissus — Narcissus

Liriope and Cephissus represent a diversified combination of projective identifications, in which one does not exist for the other. Actually, each one is *himself/herself* in the Other. That is why they have a child, Narcissus, who becomes a "nobody" and acts like such. He does not have an affection for anyone but himself. He doesn't hear or notice anything consciously. He only perceives his parents' pathological filicide, albeit unconsciously, through his *non-existence*. He is deaf to the outside world, which is represented by Echo. He tries to get cured and, upon seeing himself as a total object in the water, he also realizes that his parents have an unconscious wish that he should die. Since he didn't feel that he existed, he kills himself in an act of self-love.

At the clinic, we have some patients who say that they are "dead." I believe that the great risk of suicide is in their need to kill themselves to be sure that they were once alive.

The two stories in the chart overlap in regards to the type of affection. As a couple, Laius and Jocasta are more individually differentiated when compared to Cephissus and Liriope. The latter are completely mixed in, as we can see in the chart (one enters the other.) However, each individual in the two couples married themselves in the Other. Each one of them does what they want, while it is apparently what the Other wants because the Other is his/her own self.

Laius and Jocasta are more mature, both as individuals and as a couple, so much so that they consciously make a decision to order Oedipus' death. Liriope and Cephissus are much more disturbed; each one does not realize that the other one exists. Therefore, Narcissus' death is foretold unconsciously in their "apparent meeting."

The Myth of Narcissus and the Tragedy of Oedipus

The tragedy of Oedipus is an extension of Narcissus' myth. Let's say that, with Narcissus' death, the myth interrupts the emotional development of the protagonist in his paranoid schizophrenic position, which means that there was an introjection of partial objects—mainly the bad and destructive ones—with which Narcissus agrees due to the genetic component and his emotional development. When he sees, for a moment, both his parents and himself as total objects, he gets depressed and cannot withstand his own suicidal wishes, nor does he withstand the pathological filicide of his parents. Pathological filicide also appears in mnemic traces, which are particular to children of pathologically narcissistic parents.[24]

With Oedipus, Sophocles goes deeper into Narcissus' emotional development. He makes him survive the effective homicide attempt of his parents to, despite himself, become parricidal, marry his own mother, father his own siblings and, ultimately, commit suicide (when the earth busted open to receive him) upon knowing himself. Apparently, Oedipus made more damage to his life and that of others than Narcissus, but despite his pathological narcissism he was able to love and allow himself to be loved. He turned his libido towards the world in a "twisted" way—homicidal and suicidal—, but he was able to in-

---

24 It is not that other babies who show an adequate emotional development don't have what Freud calls "mnemic traces," that is, notions of future memory.

vest in external objects, unlike Narcissus, who lived only in his own world populated by his own suicidal mnemic traces and the pathologically filicidal impulses from his parents.

Narcissus never made contacts that did not concern him (hunting buddies), while Oedipus created bonds, despite the fact that they were paranoid ones (e.g. when he accused his brother-in-law of usurping the kingdom.) In fact, Narcissus tried to make a contact—a semi contact, that is—with Echo, the nymph, but it was actually an unsuccessful attempt to create a bond with himself. Both Narcissus and Oedipus died when they got to know themselves. However, Narcissus was more deeply ill and into himself. Consequently, let's say that he died during the "first round." Oedipus only died on the "second round" because he was able to create bonds outside himself. Tiresias revelation, when he stated that Oedipus had killed the king, his own father, triggers the transition from introjected partial objects to total objects and makes him disintegrate[25] until he kills himself, as Narcissus did.

His introjected total objects were very frail for an attempt at restoring them. Oedipus deciphered the riddle of the Sphinx. He is capable of having depressive moments like that, in which he is accompanied by real external figures. Narcissus is always alone. Oedipus gets married and has children. He knows that his parricide and incestuous situation is a psychotic one, even though

---

25 As a matter of fact, it is about "disassembling" after a deep assembling task triggered by an insight. Overall, this type of assembling lasts seconds, as we see at the clinic. Right after that, patients disassemble themselves. With the assembling task, they can't stand the pain of guilt.

only at an unconscious level, and that is why he makes all possible efforts to learn who had killed his father. He knows everything, but he keeps going on until the very end. He could have remained in denial and keep accusing his brother-in-law or someone else. But he demanded that Tiresias (his superego) utter aloud what he himself already knew, so that his superego can seek revenge. He can no longer bear the remorse, nor does he have courage or depressive moments that are sufficiently strong to take responsibility for his acts, which would have freed him from suicide. Despite the pain, he could have accomplished some restitutions.

On the other hand, Narcissus had always remained extremely alone. I believe Sophocles (496 b.C. - 406 a.D.) because of several events found throughout the narrative and mainly due to the presence of Tiresias, the blind, as an eye witness in both Oedipus' and Narcissus' tragedies, which gave Oedipus a more dramatic and mature ending from a psychoanalytical perspective.

The presence of Tiresias in both accounts, even though they were set three centuries apart as written records, leads me to believe that Sophocles took the myth of Narcissus as it was found in oral tradition in Greece to create his "Oedipus the King," while Roman poet Ovid (43 b.C. - 17 a.D.) limited himself to giving literary form to a Greek myth that, like many others, had followed a long path since its origin throughout the centuries, thus immortalizing it in his *Metamorphoses*. However, the important thing here is the interesting overlap of the two myths: Oedipus and Narcissus.

According to the *Dictionaire de Ia Mythologie*

Grecque et Romaine,[26] there were several versions to the myth of Narcissus. One of these versions called my attention precisely because it mentions the suicide of one of Narcissus' male lovers, as it had happened when Laius's male lover killed himself in the tragedy of Oedipus. This version is from Boeotia, in Greece, and it stands out for being very different from the rest:

> "Narcissus was from a city not so far away from Mount Helicon. He was a young handsome man who looked down upon love. Another young man, Ameinias, fell in love with him. Narcissus turned down his advances constantly, but finally sent him a sword as a gift. Obediently, Ameinias used it to kill himself at the doorsteps of Narcissus' house. As he was dying, Ameinias asked the Gods to curse Narcissus, and so one day it happened when Narcissus was in the forest and fell in love with himself. Desperately infatuated, he committed suicide then and there. The residents of the city organized a Love Ritual, whose power had revealed itself in that story: A flower bloomed on the ground tarnished by Narcissus' blood, and it was named after him.[27]"

Narcissus died while submerged in his father, the river, the water,[28] in an extremely lonely situation. Oe-

---

26 GRIMAL, Pierre. *Dictionaire de Ia Mythologie Grecque et Romaine*. Paris: Presses Universitaires de France, 1979

27 According to the Encyclopedia Britannica (Volume 15, 1972, Brazilian Edition), this version is an attempt at comprehending a legend that already exists.

28 This fact has a significant meaning because the water, in this case, represents the father, a castrating superego that is pathologically fili-

dipus killed his father and, taken by remorse for killing him to be with his own mother, committed suicide. It is in Narcissus' pressing solitude that Freud found support to show that pathological narcissism is not susceptible to psychoanalytical treatment because they, the patients, are the object of themselves. In turn, patients who reach their Oedipal phase, the depressive position, can be subjected to psychoanalysis according to Freud. This depressive position indicates that individuals have gone from the phase of concrete thought to that of symbolization; therefore, they are able to manage the transference process demanded by psychoanalysis upon reaching a more emotionally mature state, in which they become capable of perceiving themselves and the Other, despite the fact that, melancholically, they may still need suicide as a resource.

I would like to emphasize that I do not believe that Oedipus has lived his depressive phase in a stable manner, since even though he was capable of creating symbols, he executed parricide instead of only fantasizing with it. According to Bion, this shows that both Oedipus and Narcissus had psychotic personalities. However, Narcissus interrupted his emotional development prematurely. Overall, he did not progress from his paranoid schizophrenic phase. He tried to have the depressive moments that were abundant in Oedipus, even though Oedipus himself was only able to internalize total objects at the moment he was about to commit suicide, as it happened with Narcissus. Suicide in and of itself already has as a consequence the

cidal, which Narcissus cannot overcome in order to reach a depressive position.

internalization of total objects, because immature people would never be able to attempt suicide.

Despite a genetic legacy, suicide requires the least amount of time—let's say a millionth of a second—for individuals to see themselves and others as independent people, each one with their own feelings. Most people who are considered normal rarely perceive others because they are living in their specific realities. Consequently, Oedipus could have passed for a "normal person," but insisted in revealing his illness and punished himself for it.

FILICIDE

All families are alike. Some are worse.
Carmem Dametto

Why isn't filicide talked about freely in psychoanalysis, despite the emphasis on parricide and matricide? May it be because the feeling is worse?

Conceptualization

Filicide, whether it is pathological or not, is an inherent feeling to human nature. But we should not forget the phylogenetic legacy that acts over ontogenetics; that is, we cannot forget that we come from monkeys. Filicidal practice started with the animals that zoologically came before us. We are all aware of animals, even pets, who eat, kill, or simply leave their offspring to starve.

As far as Man as a rational animal is concerned, filicide is the unconscious or conscious desire to kill or mutilate their children, regardless of the method. I say "unconsciously" because there are thousands of ways to eliminate a child, some clearer and some more subtle than others, and that are not perceived in the analytical and psychiatric work. We will go through some of them here.

In primitive hordes, an animal fights its "son" for the females in the group; it does not simply abandon the object of its desire without any confrontation. Therefore, the father tries to kill his young, which represents the son that, in turn, tries to kill his elder, which represents the father. In *Totem and Taboo*, Freud described well the state of filicide and parricide in primitive hordes. However, when addressing Oedipus Complex at a later time, Freud only put emphasis on the parricidal son without mentioning filicide, which he did for reasons only he himself would know. He was unable to or uninterested in observing how Oedipus' parents had tried to kill him as well.

Filicide, whether it is pathological or not, appears constantly in history, religion, and corporations such as the Army, associations, and other group activities. Of course it receives parricide, matricide, or even fratricide in return. However, I would like to limit myself to filicide, whether it is pathological or not, because it has become taboo in clinical psychoanalysis. The subject is not addressed; therefore, it does not exist. Consequently, it is not treated along with pathological *narcissism*, thus making psychoanalysis a tool to curtail feelings considered undesirable, despite inherent to human beings.

At the psychiatric practice office, there is a risk of mistaking the role of the therapist with that of a representative of the superego for a determined society and culture, so as to produce in the patient a *false self* or, in case of reluctance, the risk of labeling him "resistant to analysis."

The fact of the matter is that, if we do not analyze this deep interrelation between parents and children within narcissism and its implications—filicide, suicide, parricide, matricide, fratricide, and incest—we will not be able to see patients as human beings, but as a self-professed demigods, without serious life-and-death problems to resolve. I'm not referring to the demigods or gods from the Olympus, because they had no scruples when it came to ordering the death or mutilation of their children, parents, siblings, or foes.

Back to conceptualization, and according to my observations during clinical practice, filicide is *the desire felt, thought of, or acted upon to kill or mutilate a son or daughter,* as the result of a narcissistic relationship, whether it is normal or pathological, that has been established between people within a family group. In other words, filicide is the conscious desire (thought of) or unconscious desire (acted upon) of mutilating or killing a son or daughter.

Within a normal family group, the death wish of one or another member of the family is only *felt, experienced, and thought of.* Therefore, it is not *performed.* The situation is unresolved at the mental level, with all developments of remorse and blame that must be elaborated in order not to have them pushed back to the unconscious mind where they first originated. They are feelings and thoughts the individual is aware of and has painfully experienced, whether or not they were elaborated. This is normal filicide, which mandatorily calls for restitutions.

On the other hand, when a family group has pathological narcissism issues—that is, when nobody sees anybody else but themselves, for they see only themselves in the other—, the homicidal wish is so strong that it must remain hidden, because thinking of it could become, "Thought of, acted upon it." In such case, filicide is a feeling that resides in the unconscious mind and, without a relief valve, there is a great possibility that it can be effectively acted upon on several different ways, whether or not it is supported by the patients themselves, who would then carry out the act in the form of suicide. Limiting myself to my clinical or hospital experiences, many therapists wind up becoming filicidal without noticing it, because they failed to realize that, for example, had a patient been admitted to a hospital, suicide would have been prevented.

Throughout my almost thirty years of work with outpatients, interacting with psychotic individuals and psychotic family groups, I am convinced that working basically with the patient is not enough. Whenever possible and with extra care, we also need to work with the family group, the *pathologically narcissistic core of filicide*—parricide, matricide, fratricide, suicide. Otherwise, it is very difficult to achieve an effective improvement for the patient and, as I said before, it may even lead to the formation of a false self that is filled with partial objects, instead of total ones, as Melanie Klein has perceived it.

Acting in an isolated manner would be the same as perpetrating a true *pathological filicide*: Patients commit suicide or are mutilated in the most diverse of ways, be it physically or mentally. The most severe aspect of it is when pathological filicide is committed by therapists themselves. I insist that pathological filicide is practiced by psychotic individuals. It is in no way the case of psychopaths who are allegedly psychotic, as stated by their attorneys, in order to plead innocent when accused of a crime. I am not diminishing the severity and the consequences of a homicidal act, whether it is performed by someone who is having a psychotic episode or is a member of a psychotic groups. What I wish to clarify is that, in the case of common criminals, their killing is premeditated or somehow anticipated. This never happens with psychotic individuals. It is not death that makes a difference, but their motivation.

For example, psychotic patients may be agitated during an episode and, while unaware of their strength, push someone that may be fatally wounded. That is what I call a psychotic homicide, which is different from a homicidal psychotic who could just as well be a homicidal diabetic, a homicidal asthmatic, and so on and so forth. Cases of plain homicide belong to the police scope. Unfortunately, these individuals can get a *habeas corpus* easily. I will address the subject when we discuss social filicide, that is, genocide.

We must emphasize the cases in which filicide does not need to be perpetrated. Once again, conscious filicidal desire is a normal human feeling. Parents aren't always prepared emotionally or socially when they have a child. Therefore, it is only natural that they think of their child as a burden, someone who should not exist. However, they treat the child as an Other, an individual who was born despite their will (consciously), but nevertheless needs care.

When filicide is thought about this way, it attacks

the parents' narcissism so strongly that the issue is resolved by itself.

How is filicide resolved?

With displays of affections and disaffection, even at inappropriate times. In normal individuals, there is always an affective bond that unites parents and their children. It is with this contact that filicide can be "resolved." The same will not happen in abnormal cases, in which this link was never formed or has been broken for some reason. In such scenario there will be no continuous exchange of affection, only sporadic ones that do not take parents and children towards a relationship that will make introjection possible, whether this introjection is of parental figures or social rules.

Why does filicide appear?

I'd like to recall what I wrote back in 1981 regarding the formation of a pathologically narcissistic couple in my book *Personalidade Psicótica e Psicose*, under a section of the "Oedipus at the Crossroads" chapter. Once they inherit the pathology, children may be born genetically with a mission to accomplish: To kill or mutilate themselves. No matter the method, they will be following the unconscious intentions of their paternal figures, despite their partial objects. The phenomenon is very clear in the myth of Narcissus. Cephissus, the river, shows no scruples upon learning that nymphs have no desire to have "sexual relations" with him. I'm not sure we can call it that way since, for what we understand of "sexual relations," there was no involvement at the genital level, not even with Liriope. In turn, Liriope thinks narcissistically that the river (Cephissus) will treat her with respect and it couldn't be any other way. However, she gets pregnant and becomes the mother of Narcissus.

In our analytical practice, it is common to observe someone who falls madly in love with someone else, but it never goes beyond the appearances. Instead of having a psychotic episode, individuals "fall in love," projecting their identifications on the other, who may or may not have mutual feelings. If this love is corresponded, they will create a pathologically narcissistic couple. As a matter of fact, each one "falls in love" with himself/ herself in the other. Therefore, there is no affective bond. This is what happens with teenagers, when they have a long relationship from the time they are thirteen, fifteen years old, for example. Let's say they then get married when they are twenty-something. They have a child and soon are separated. I call this a "psychiatric internment"[29] with an unhappy ending for a baby who, upon being born, usually brings the "couple" to reality.

I call it "internment" even during sessions with patients at my practice, in order to show them that they

29 Both are ill and each one acts like to other one's "nurse" or a canvas into which they can project whatever they wish.

are interested only in getting rid of the illness (psychosis), cannot have a mature relationship yet, and are unable to see their partners as the Other Person. At a more advanced age, separations and divorces are also common for the same reasons. The children have grown up and husband and wife realize that there is nothing else left to unite them. Actually, there never was. When they get divorced, they once again repeat the cycle, having successive "marriages" in which their partners are either similar to them—thus creating a pathologically narcissistic couple—or in the best-case scenario, a new partner who is a transitional object for the individual leaving the "relationship."

According to Winnicott, a transitional object would be something that, despite external to the individual, is a possession and serves to diminish his or her own angst. It is the typical case of having a favorite teddy bear, pillow, or blanket like Linus from Charlie Brown. Many people cannot face loneliness and try to mask it with a "marriage." So, when the relationship is over, they soon look for a similar partner to restore their internal balance, which is something they can achieve in the short term while creating a revolving door with a long string of sporadic transitional objects.

It is important to notice that pathological narcissists attract pathological narcissists, with direct mass measurements, as Newton would say.

Why do I talk about an attack on narcissism?

There is normal narcissism, which someone acquires throughout their existence. Individuals accept life as it is, even if at first they are frightened by what is new. What is *new* is always an attack on the level of narcissism that a normal person may have been able to reach, thus overcoming its potentially related pathologies.

In Freud's work, the notion of narcissism varies according to the text, since he always has something else to add. At first, he said that narcissism—which he called something secondary—is a state in which the libido withdrawn within the ego becomes objectified, that is, it is placed in the external world. It is an instinct of self-preservation, a vital need that can become harmful in excess, though.[30] One example of such state is when patients get ill during their first attempt of seeking a cure. This way, we can understand the behavior of a pathologically narcissistic, schizophrenic patient, whom I will refer to here as psychotic.

Freud also considers narcissism to be inherent to human beings, as the act of admiring and being proud of oneself, for instance. In fact, he reaches a conclusion that, I believe, is more definite as far as I have understood it.

At a certain point, narcissism—or rather, libidinous investment in the ego—helps to resolve affections at the mental level when they once were resolved at the physical level. For it to happen, leaving the physical (auto-erotic) to the mental level, a psychological act has to take

---

30 Megalomania, for example.

place. Once again, as far as I have understood it, this new psychological act is narcissism, which triggers the beginning of the formation of ego at the mental level, with the sturdy use of its basic defense mechanisms—projective and introjective identifications, dissociation, and repression—and the subsequent the formation of partial objects. All that, obviously, from the neurological development of babies and the use they will make of their genetic legacy.[31]

Ego is formed as a consequence of a collision of id and the outside world, which starts to take place at birth, not at a conscious knowledge level, but in terms of physical well-being and ill-being. It is about recognizing what belongs to your own body, which leads to ego differentiation. If a baby's narcissism is pathological—that is, if the baby does not perceive or welcome what comes from an external source, or rather receives it as an attack and starts to "withdraw within herself"—this baby will be a severely ill patient in the future. *Her pathological narcissism is a genetic legacy from her pathologically narcissistic parents, that is, this baby is the offspring of a marriage that did not take place, as I mentioned earlier. Each individual married himself or herself in the other while apparently forming a couple.*

In pathological narcissism, there is no objectivation of libido. By "libido," I perceive all affection investments regarding ourselves and the outside world, which can be of a love or hate nature—or of life or death. If narcissists become ill after having already objectified their

---

31 Please refer to the difference between a baby with a psychotic personality and a baby with a non-psychotic personality, which is the subject of *Personalidade Psicótica e Psicose*, the book I wrote in 1981.

affection, they will withdraw within their ego again and become the object of themselves, as Freud used to say. Therefore, talking about narcissism is not about addressing a disease, but a possible cured disease.

Yes, humans are narcissistic and being narcissistic is necessary. It is when facing obstacles in life that we see how each one of us was able to resolve our own pathological narcissism. Before a son or daughter, narcissism is put to the test every single second. In the beginning, parents are completely ignorant of the new being; parents and baby are strangers and will have to be introduced to one another. Nobody can tell for sure whether they'll get along. Despite planned, the new being comes between the relationship of these two individuals. The new being (if it is indeed a *new being*) will always put parents in check for as long as they live—and may the dead not hear us, maybe even after their death.

For example, when a mother arrives from work and finds her son crying, she may think, *"Why the hell does this child exist?"* However, such reaction comes only to mind and this mother inevitably will take an action in favor of or against the child, but always *in regards to the child.* She does it while driven by remorse or guilt for being angry, whether her reaction comes in the short or long term. With each "fight," if the mother progressively becomes aware of each other's participation in the event—both hers and the child's—and is capable of reducing them to their true importance, there will be a less threatening affection bond and the child will start using memory from repression.

For example, by taking her son in her arms and

soothing him, the mother will be helping the child to go from the paranoid schizophrenia position to the depressive position at a given moment. Very young children use their own mnemic traces as a small computer to save data regarding the way that their mothers function and their own reactions to the affection they receive. I'm talking about babies with normal emotional development (*abnormal* babies only compute the data they wish to compute), whose mothers also have the ability of stepping outside themselves to look at the situation from a different perspective, evaluate their own feelings and correct them. Children who adequately form their ego will have good subsidies for future encounters with their mother and, somehow, also start to develop a response that is aligned with this type of behavior: This is the beginning of an *affective bond* between mother and child.

If the mother has an unfavorable reaction to the child, that is, if she tells the son off instead of comforting him, nothing I've said above will change, as long as the child is able to benefit from each conflict and starts to know more about himself from their dynamics. The important thing is that there will be a meeting between them, so that they can create a *bond*.[32]

The behavior of a mother that acts that way, because she is tired or does not feel well, is considered normal. She lives in reality, she knows her limits, she realizes that she is shaken at a given moment and is aware that she

---

32 The eventual anger does not necessarily overcome the love that a mother has for her child. When these feelings come to the surface, the child will comprehend that she is loved and acknowledge that her mother is not a goddess.

herself has problems; she does not feel narcissistically attacked by the child. For better or worse, she thinks about and feels the existence of *another being*. She is "bothered," in the sense of being affected by the other, the child.

She, the mother, exists. He, the son, also exists. They are two people and the affective situation between the two of them needs to be resolved. The child, in turn, needs to learn how to respect the other's reality. For him, the effect of his mother's reaction isn't very different in one case or another. The important thing for the child is that his own feelings of love and hate in regards to his mother are able to surface and be recognized by himself, whether they are accepted or not. On the other hand, the mother only allows herself to externalize her anger, without any uneasiness, when she feels that her love is bigger than her anger.

Actually, quoting Winnicott, who dedicated himself so much to the affective bonds between mother and child, the first feeling that a normal mother experiences upon having a child is hate. Here's the explanation: First of all, her body is deformed, then she loses a piece of herself, that is, the child she grew inside of her. She feels labor pains, which is common. She foresees the hard work ahead of her. She goes from the "pregnant" *status* to the "unhappy mother" *status*, which some say is good, but "lasts too long." As a consequence of the birth, many have emotional reactions that may range from milder issues (insomnia, slight agitation, a little depression, crying spells) to deeper issues, such as postpartum psychosis. That is why many women who fear natural child birth, which may put their physical and/or mental integrity at risk, would rather have a C-section. In the case of postpartum psychosis, the mother is already ill before the birth. When her child is born, along with all the aforementioned losses, it triggers a psychotic crisis.

Also as mentioned above, filicide is manifested in different ways in "normal people" as well. Normally, it is expected that an affective bond be formed from the very first minute of interactions between mother and child. I suspect that something like that could never happen, since the baby does not have an *ego* capable of such a thing. This is what I see from a psychotic patient at the hospital, who only after many years of adequate treatment has become aware that something must have happened to him as a child that he was unable to enjoy, either due to his own deficiencies or because his mother was unable to transmit it to him.

Considering the above, we cannot think about narcissism in terms of formation of ego, superego, and mnemic traces, but only in terms of *potentialities* that may be realized for better or worse in the future, and only in the case of children with a perfect sensorial perception, because any disorder in this area will affect all other perceptions as consequence.[33] We know that a child's central nervous system takes years to operate completely. And sensorial perception requires a normal nervous system in order to develop properly.[34] A blind or deaf child will

33 For example, a mosquito bites a baby and, due to a twisted sensorial perception, the baby introjects the idea that it was her mother who hurt her.

34 This is not intended to mean that babies can only develop their egos after having a mature nervous system. However, their emotional de-

hardly be able to receive 100% of the stimuli provided by the mother.

velopment will be easier if the respective notions are within normal standards.

Forms of Filicide

This chapter will address *normal* and *pathological* types of filicide, as well as some ways in which both are present.

Filicide goes through the head of parents and children (as ideation). Therefore, filicide is thought of by people whom we could label as normal, and it happens at different levels, from the "Dammit! I can't go to the movies because of this child" to a more extreme "Why doesn't this child just die, so I can be free?" that comes in a moment of wrath due to an act perpetrated by the child.

One of the normal forms of filicide, for example, is thinking about aborting a child. I believe this is the first thing that crosses the minds of an unprepared couple, that is, two people who do not wish to have a child at that moment in their lives. An *abnormal* form of filicide is when a couple had been preparing for an eventual pregnancy and, when it does take place, decide to have an abortion[35] after feeling that it would be a threatening event.

---

35 However, this couple may have acted normally when considering an abortion if they realized that their marriage was over and that a child would only "unite" them once again.

In fact, in the case of a pathologically narcissistic couple, the birth of a child could be the cause of a "break-up," as the narcissistic relationship between husband and wife comes undone and is replaced by the narcissistic relationship between mother and child. The father is left to the side, a third wheel. The "couple" is broken. There are only a man and a woman without any matrimonial bond. Even if the "couple" is unaware of it, the "family" is no longer. It has lost its reason for being. There are only three people who depend on one another.

In the case of marriages between pathologically narcissistic individuals, they lose what we call "role" as in "husband's role" and "wife's role." With the birth of the child and the withdrawal of libido from the father (now ex-father) or the mother (now ex-mother), the "family" will remain apparently formed by the "couple" and the "child." However, they are three people without an affective bond amongst themselves. Each individual withdraws their own affection within themselves.

Sometimes, a new couple can be formed between father and child or mother and child; even husband and wife could become a couple again. But the thing is that one of the three will become the "third wheel" in the affective bond and the three will be dependent-independent beings in relation to one another, making believe that they are a family, that is, a couple with a child.

Another form of *normal* filicide is to think and desire the child not to be born, thus getting rid of the burden that the child represents, regardless of the child being healthy or not, perfect and beautiful or not. The individuals in this couple have already reached the depressive position talked about by Melanie Klein: Father and Mother are susceptible to feeling guilty for having considered abortion and make an attempt of reparation by providing care to the baby.[36] In addition to the treatment of the body (feeding, personal hygiene, etc.), it is probable that they also transmit notions of boundaries and respect towards others, and demand that the baby treat them well in return.

Good parents aren't the ones who "allow" their children to do whatever they want. Likewise, they practice *pathological filicide* as well. A child who is raised indiscriminately cannot develop normally. This child will become an ill individual. Babies need parameters at all times, so that they can form (develop) their ego and grow as mentally healthy individuals. That is no small task and demands that parents be healthy and certain of their love for their child. That is the only way they can allow themselves to say *no* when needed and *yes* in due time, thus building an imaginary path that the child must follow, a path that has one lane marked "yes" and another lane marked "no."

After walking down the proper Yes and No lanes, babies can go through the hard path of *Perhaps*, which they will have to follow throughout the rest of their lives, going from a paranoid schizophrenia position to a depressive position.[37] Only ill individuals are 100% sure of everything all the time. We must doubt our convictions

---

36 This care is provided by the father to the mother, then by both to the baby, with the additional care of setting boundaries.
37 This holding environment described by Winnicott is also known as "mothering bond."

whenever the opportunity presents itself, which normally happens all the time. Doubt is one of the prerogatives of Man as a rational animal.

That is why, during treatment sessions, I must change at all times so as to make patients think; otherwise the situation would become *static*, without life's dynamic interactions. That doesn't mean that the one and only point of treatment is taking patients down a path of constant doubt about everything, for this would create the perfect conditions for a psychotic confusion crisis. The main thing is providing patients and therapists the possibility, the *certainty of being able to double-guess convictions* without going mad.[38]

In regards to the variety and amount of normal forms of filicide, there are as many ways to execute it as *human thoughts and feelings permit*; therefore, the same amount and diversity of thoughts and feelings may exist. Since thoughts and feelings are free and endless, there are infinite forms of filicide. In our daily lives, filicide goes from hating your child to thinking about drowning or breaking her neck. But these are only wishes that are "thought of" and *never acted upon*. That which is thought of and never acted upon remains in the realm of normality because they assume a very large ego capacity from the part of the mother or father, which is in their thinking and feeling something and being able to rework their unfair feelings or thoughts—referred to as "*gauche*"—with other

---

38 When individuals have nothing but doubts, they are ill. On the other hand, if they are sure of everything, they are just as ill. Extreme convictions are classified in the paranoid schizophrenic position of "I am God," which undoubtedly is delusional.

thoughts or feelings that lead to reparation, in the sense that Melanie Klein attributes to it.

Example: A mother is at the supermarket with her son, who throws a temper-tantrum because he wants a toy. The mother starts out by saying, "No." People stare at mother and son—or at one or the other. The mother loses control and slaps the son, but still doesn't buy the toy. She regrets having slapped him, then she feels guilty. Finally, she apologizes, explaining how both could have acted better. The situation is explicit.[39] The mother said "No" and the child will have to learn how to deal with frustration, because it is better that it comes from the mother, during childhood, than later on *in real life*.

It is important to warn parents that filicide is perceived by the child as it takes place. As a response, the child may return the feeling with parricide or matricide. If his ego is developing well, these feelings will be absorbed normally by his superego, an unconscious internal instance in charge of fiercely punishing such events in case the child doesn't feel comfortable with him and/or his parents.

How many children dream that they are killing their mother or father and calmly tell them that when they wake up? They can do so because their relationship is good, going through an invisible thread in which many positive things can be thought of and experienced, but

---

39 I believe there is a difference between remorse and guilt. Remorse is related to the paranoid schizophrenic phase and to partial objects. Guilt implies a depressive phase and total objects. A normal person experiences paranoid schizophrenic moments as well as depressive moments.

not acted upon.

However, it is not a child's pure mind that makes her tell her parents about such dreams. It is her mental health, her ego that was structured on a solid foundation and the certainty of a holding environment of acceptance, without triggering a response as "Oh, that's horrible! How can you dream about a thing like that? I take such good care of you!" Children who fear hearing their parents say something similar wouldn't tell them their own thoughts, dreams, and desires, nor would they share their doubts with them. They would already be a little or very ill.

Children who realize filicide and then retaliate with matricide or parricide are free from feelings of suicide, which is the accumulation of hate towards oneself upon noticing an attack from their parents. This means that they do not feel omnipotent and narcissistically that powerful to the point that they carry all the hate from the trio—father, mother, and child. Therefore, they are babies and children who have a well-structured ego, who perceive or experience other people in the world, and know that they have a Mommy and a Daddy.

As a matter of fact, babies still can't "feel" in the same meaning that we attribute to the word "to feel." Let's say that they have an uncomfortable feeling that their physical integrity is being threatened, a notion of annihilation and mutilation that, later, appears in psychotic adults and in individuals who have a false *self*. Since they don't have well-structured egos, nor do they have a memory of the event, they only carry the feeling they experienced, but without being aware of it. When they do acquire the knowledge, it is as if they were delusional upon externalizing it.

A patient of mine used to always say, "My parents want me to die." It sounded delusional, but I knew that wasn't the case. He also had some suicidal thoughts mixed in with this "affection confusion," and was unable to get rid of them, so he turned all these feelings towards himself. One fine day, I decided to confirm to him that his parents did indeed wish him dead and that he agreed with them. He never repeated that sentence, which in other hospitals would have been considered delusional and sufficient motive to subject him to shock therapy. It is true that he was very shocked with my confirmation, but I was able to explain to him that it was only a piece of information, so that he could separate the feelings coming from him from those who came unconsciously from his parents.

This event is different from another case of a female patient whose father had clearly told her, "You have to commit suicide." She didn't follow through, simply because she wasn't in a position to "hear" it. Her *ego* wasn't sufficiently structured for her to listen to such a monstrous thing without indeed killing herself. Had she reached a paranoid schizophrenic position, she could have effectively committed suicide in one of those moments of integration that lead to a depressive position. However, her ego was still so divided that she could have either heard her father's orders and simply been unable to *listen* to him, or she was able to hear it and then *reacted* by trying to attack or successfully attacking other patients or therapists. She was then defending herself from an aggression that was unknown to her; she attacked others to defend herself, for those were filicide and parricide attempts even though she was unaware of the facts.

There was a child that I treated who had been abandoned by her father as a baby. At seven years of age, she had a dream that he wanted to kill her with a machine gun. I asked what she thought of it and she said, "I thought of killing him too." That is an absolutely normal attitude, a result of her *knowledge* and acceptance of her father's abandoning her (pathological filicide), something she had to retaliate with parricide without any guilt. Other patients had expressed in a "delusional" way the most diversified types of mutilation they had endured—I say "delusional" using quotation marks because I believe they somehow have been effectively mutilated, without knowing it, because of hunger, thirst, pain, or lack of maternal love. They feel half-dead and, to prove to themselves that they are alive, they often resort to self-mutilation or suicide.

One of my patients had the feeling that "part of flesh in my arms and legs flies away and stays on the outside, with the soul." But he doesn't feel anxious about it, because anxiety is a very mature feeling for him to experience. He simply reported his experience as if it were a mere fact, then he added, "My father treats me very badly." He is the son of parents who have been divorced since he was a small child. Maybe there is a connection between these two confessions, but this is something I'll only know for sure in about ten years or so in the best-case scenario.

One very common form of pathological filicide that we often find during treatment with psychotic individuals is when parents realize that their child (the patient) and the therapist have created a bond, even the slightest one, and then try to destroy it. How do they do it? Unconsciously, they try to irritate therapists, putting them against their children. If therapists aren't well aware of these devices, it is only natural that they'll allow to be influenced by the anger that these parents have towards their children, thus treating their patients with less care. The only thing these parents think they can do when they're jealous of this bond between a patient and a therapist is to sever it, to incite anger in one side (patient) or the other (therapist), or maybe even both. They resort to several maneuvers, the most common of them being an attack to the therapist's competence.

I know of a case that would be funny, had it not been offensive. A father wanted to terminate his son's treatment prematurely. However, he did not have any justifiable reason to do so. The only excuse was that he had to keep his schizophrenic child home to entertain his wife (and make her life hell) while he, the father, could enjoy his extramarital relationship. As a womanizer, he didn't think twice and started to attack the therapist and suggested that his son should be treated by younger, prettier professionals. The thing is that these treatment sessions never lasted longer than a year.

I believe these things happen, in part, due to the reservations that therapists have in reporting such unconsciously macabre maneuvers, which are lethal to patients. I report them all. I say, "Your parents want to kill you. If you agree with them, then it's okay! I just won't buy it that I can't treat you just because I'm ugly."

I remember I had a patient once who was a drug addict and I always showed his parents' maneuvers to him. One day, he realized his mother used to "unintentionally" leave money next to bed. He told me, "She wants me to buy cocaine, but I didn't take the money." When the patient had already got clean and improved his case of schizophrenia, his parents decided to admit him. He then called me from the hospital, saying that it was no use doing anything against those parents of his. He committed suicide.

Another schizophrenic patient sent me a letter telling me she was going to jump out of the window. She had been my patient, but her brother was a doctor and believed he could treat her better with his methods and removed her from treatment. When I received her letter, I called her mother, who did nothing. The patient did throw herself from her window and died.

Many times you need to introduce treatment elements little by little, so that patients can put them together and reach an adequate conclusion. As patients make progress during treatment, I start to place the latent material right before them, so that they can acknowledge them, put them together, and then have their own insights. This way, I try to prevent any pain of having someone (me) communicate something at a time when they will be unable to withstand it, which would be filicide on my part, for I would be pushing patients away from me and our treatment.

***

Clinical Session

A patient told me she was afraid I wouldn't agree with her job options. In fact, I didn't, but I wouldn't tell her that to avoid a head collision that could push her away from dialog. I found a way around it instead.

Carmem: You may not adapt well to that job, but don't be frightened, because you can try out other jobs.

Patient: I know I'm capable of experimenting with many others.

C: We don't know it yet, because you haven't tried it. Let's take it easy.

P: It'll work! [She starts to second-guess herself.] Well, I'll go and see if I can do it, right?

C: That's right. If you can't, that's not the end of the world.

P: But they want someone who can type and I can't.

C: Maybe they'll like other things that you can do.

P: You know what, Carmem? I'm not capable enough to take this job. I'll look for another job. Will you help me?

This is the end of the important part of this example. The main thing is that you can't tell a psychotic individual something that will make them feeling worse than they already do. It would be pointless. In the aforementioned case, I won't be hurting a patient by saying, "You're not capable enough," because she already knows it. However, it would just hurt her pathological narcissism, while she can reach that conclusion all by herself, as I helped her do, without pushing her away from me, our treatment, and her health. Pathologically narcissistic individuals can only hear what they already know (unconsciously). I can't do what their superego does in this phase, which is reached narcissistically, completely primitively and in a castrating way. We know that, when ego comes undone in psychotic cases, superego crumbles even faster and attacks patients from inside out, punishing them for being ill and not allowing them to become better or accept help.

The ego becomes inactive and the superego becomes hyperactive, punishing patients who had the guts to go mad. For example, it makes patients feel dead inside or attempt suicide. It demands that they work or study without having any condition to do so. Many therapists don't notice this sadistic maneuver made by their superego, which is attacked in its narcissism, and "tease" patients with things that are impossible for them to do at the moment, thus amplifying their illness. That is when the distance between therapist and patients begins to grow.

One thing is having patients talk about what they can do; what they have the ability to actually do at a given moment is another story. This is something that must be evaluated and worked in a non-pathological way by the therapist. For example, I used to supervise a colleague who was motivating his psychotic patient to go live by himself. I realized he was working with his patient at a conversational level, not at the patient's true capabilities—he was in the paranoid schizophrenic phase. And, while this therapist thought the patient was "ready to be discharged and go leave by himself," the patient couldn't work or study, not even read the paper. What would he do in an apartment all by himself?

***

It seems filicide is either a taboo and cannot be put into words by therapists, or they are simply unable to identify it. A therapist who does not address filicide and, consequently, parricide, matricide, fratricide, incest, and pathological narcissism cannot treat a psychotic patient or people with a false self. These therapists will never be able to help psychotic individuals to form their ego.

A parent's wish that their child did not exist can be *experienced* by a baby, who may express it years later through a mental illness or simply a realization such as "I don't feel I exist," or "I feel empty," or "I don't feel my own body." I have heard from hospital patients statements such as "I'm dead, Doctor Carmem"—especially from individuals who had been admitted to a dynamic guidance clinic where I used to work at during shifts or within the Operational Group I coordinated. Apparently, these are delusional ideas, only words, absurd expressions from parents. Yes, they are "delusional ideas," but only in part. Their parents wished that their child died, and this wish was unconsciously perceived and brought in genetically by this patient, who did wish to die.

In *Delusion and Dream in Jensen's Gradiva* (1907), Freud introduced clearly the meaning and genesis of delusion. Some patients confessed to me that their parents really wanted them to die. However, as one of them said, things like that cannot be uttered at a traditional hospital, "otherwise they'll come with the Haldol injection." In fact, this patient's parents wanted him to die, but his ambivalent scale tilted to the side of life. This is where the genetic composition of each individual comes into play to determine the use of what they've received from their parents, who in turn have already received twisted affection information.

As another patient of mine says, the hardest part is to "say things," referring to the treatment in that "I don't use interpretations." Indirectly, I tell patients what they would like to expose, but "hide" in their unconscious mind. I am careful not to allow them to see through my tactics, so as to not hurt their pathological narcissism. Here's an example:

"Your mother had a hard time getting closer to you, didn't she?"

"That's true, she did, so I couldn't get closer to her."

No narcissistic patient wants to hear something that is not exclusively about *themselves*. They only accept it if it apparently comes from themselves (patients). If patients have a good holding environment with their therapist, to the point that the therapist can say something very painful to them—such as the fact the they weren't loved by their mother, or that they were loved and couldn't notice it—there will be a discussion regarding that fact that will guide them towards realizing many problems they didn't know they had.

A few years ago, I had a teenage girl in treatment. I always forgot her name when I had to write it down in my calendar. That fact started to bother me, because I had realized that she was unconsciously communicating her non-existence to me in a way that was full of projective identifications. I was afraid of telling her that, because her father had committed suicide and she could do it too.

Her first name wasn't hers; it was the female version of her father's name. One day I took the risk and asked her.

Carmem: Patient, do you by any chance have this feeling that you don't exist?

Patient: Are you nuts, Carmem? Where did that come from?

C: My calendar. [I then explained what had been happening.]

P: That's all I've ever felt my entire life; that I don't exist. First, I don't have a name. Then my father kills himself. Worse, my mother says she only has a son. She's always forgotten about me and can only remember my brother.

Having twins or being a twin can also be perceived as filicide. I have had the opportunity throughout the years to work, treat, or live with sets of twins, as we'll see in another chapter.

A very subtle way to void the existence of a child

as such, that is, as a whole person—which is something wisely forbidden by the Jewish culture—is to repeat the name of forefathers who are still alive. If the child has the same name as someone else, she will certainly never be seen by her mother and father as a complete object. She will eventually become the depositary of the pathological narcissism of her mother or father, or maybe both. Some people have monstrous names from the combination of their parents' names. For example, Lindomar, the son of Lindolfo and Mariana. Does Lindomar exist? He will have to fight very hard against the pathological desire of his parents regarding his non-existence. What about Junior? What is he, who is he? The Second, the Son, the Grandson—do they exist? Or are they only good to remind us that someone lived before them and became immortal at the expense of the non-existence of those who inherited their name?

A very common form of pathological filicide is miscarriage and—even more, I believe—sterility. This is the apex of pathological filicide, since it comes from autoeroticism itself, it comes from the body and doesn't go through the mind. The body itself takes care of killing babies even before forming eggs or sperm. However, people repair it by adopting children *who are not theirs*. With the ability to raise a child, these people prove to themselves that they are not as destructive as they once fantasized about and are then free to conceive their own children. They already know that they will not kill them concretely.

There is also the mutilation of a child. It is common for parents to hinder the growth of a child in their social or academic development. I'd like to mention the case of a female patient who had an enormous potential as a musician. One day, she told her mother that her piano teacher had told her that she could become a concerto player one day. Her mother immediately removed her from the class, saying "You're learning piano to be a nice young lady." The patient never got close to a piano again and was an accomplice to her mother in what became an intellectual "self-mutilation." Once again, I'm only addressing mental mutilations and deaths here; I do not talk about physical mutilations and deaths, which in addition to the mental side, also have a criminal side.

Parents with a more severe pathological narcissism are, in general and in my view, the parents of future drug addicted individuals. I have written in detail about drug addiction in *Personalidade Psicótica e Psicose*.[40] However, I wanted to add some supporting facts for the identification of everything that can be toxic and present the subject in a clearer manner. I classify toxic substances as legal and illegal, so that it is clear that the notion of toxic substances is a wide one, going from water to poison.

I had a curious experience with a severe patient who attempted suicide several times by constantly ingesting water, which could result in an irreversible hydroelectrolytic imbalance in her system if she weren't under constant surveillance.

---

40 DAMETTO, Carmem. *Op. Cit.*

Legal Toxic Substances

- Substances considered harmless, such as water, but that are misused to lead to death
- Sugar can lead to obesity, heart failure, diabetes, etc.
- Alcohol can lead to neurological problems, cirrhosis, and even death
- Work in excess causes stress and death
- Smoking causes circulatory problems, cancer, and death
- Corruption leads to crime
- Medication; if it is misused, it can cause death, even if it's an antipyretic
- Shoe repair glue can lead to death
- Others, such insecticide, poison, bleach

Illegal Toxic Substances

- Cocaine, in its different methods of use
- Marijuana (pot)
- Heroin and its byproducts
- Amphetamines
- LSD
- Hashish
- Mescaline
- Others.

It's interesting when you realize that the list of licit toxic substances is larger than that of illegal ones. Another factor we must take into account is that, behind a teenage drug addict there is always, in general, a mother and/or father who is addicted to licit drugs. Or maybe it is a father who works too much and then has some beer later, or an obese mother who keeps taking diet pills and "working out" all days long. In other words, mother and father are looking at themselves too much, and not at the child.

CREATING AN AFFECTIVE BOND

How do you know if someone has an affective bond with the other?

From the time two people are in contact, it is possible to verify if there is a long-lasting or a superficial affective bond between them.

When a long-lasting relationship is formed, it creates what I call an "affective bond." That is a relationship between two whole people, with internalized total objects. However, it could happen that only one of the two people is in this stage (internalized total objects). If these people *are apart* for a period of time, despite how long that period might be, their bond remains; it doesn't need to be recreated at each meeting.

In the case of a *broken affective bond*, we can also identify whether the relationship was *definite or fleeting*. If it is definite, it is as if the bond were a power cable and there was either a short circuit or one of the people pulled the plug from the wall. It may be that the person who severed the relationship may reestablish it upon understanding the other person better, maybe forgiving her. It may also be that, after thinking things over, this person reaches the conclusion (several depressive moments) that the bond was not worth it anymore. This is the situation when friendships and marriages come to an end. In these cases, there's no turning back. Even if these two people meet again, their interaction is ephemeral and superficial, as the glossy shine of a good education. The bond no longer exists or, in the best-case scenario, it is created and destroyed at each encounter.

In the case of broken friendships, if one of the individuals is more mature and notices that the other has broken their bond due to fragility, the former may keep an open door for a potential future encounter. This may also happen in the mother-and-child relationship. The child may have a disagreement with the mother, but the mother is ready to welcome her child, unless her emotional balance is compromised as well—in such event, the internal disconnection will be definite. The door is then closed for good, even if it apparently looks like it's still open. *This is the case of a psychotic relationship between mother and child.* In the best-case scenario, it is a paranoid schizophrenic relationship.

When I mention affection relation, I'm referring to the relationship between whole individuals, with completely internalized objects. With pathological filicide, there is an obstacle. The mother was unable to remove these obstacles to provide the baby this holding environment that she needs. Going back and forth between love and hate is something that must have an *object* (mother) that welcomes such affective movements, so that the child will be sure that the mother who loves her is the same one who hates her. Babies must also return affection to their mothers.

I don't believe there is such a thing as a mother who takes care of a child, considering all the implications therein, without expecting anything in return in terms of satisfaction, but many state exactly the opposite. In fact, these mothers are the ones who feel narcissistically attacked, for example, by the unaccomplishments of their children, even though they do not realize it. Actually, they suffer a great deal when they become aware of it. Their suffering goes to the unconscious mind and, then, she either becomes a super mother or a negligent one, which in mental health terms are the one and the same. It is a psychotic relationship and it doesn't indicate an interaction between beings who are seen and perceived as *total objects*, but people who have many *projective identifications* that are "made up" according to what one expects from the other.

A psychotic relationship between mother and child is almost—but not necessarily—the same as pathological filicide because the mother may change herself, or be changed by life or treatment. Then the *door* will be opened once again and the bond will then *exist*. On the other hand, the child is already psychotic and, even if she is genetically affected and has a predisposition for schizophrenia, may try to rebuild the bond with the mother, thus changing the course of her life when looking for treatment, for example.

A good treatment is the one that works at the service of the mother-and-child bond, instead of the so-called "independence" that everybody talks about, which in reality is the confirmation signed off by therapists that all three parties—mother, child, and therapist—are incompetent at resuming the affective bond that had either existed in the past and has been broken, but could be recreated, or has never existed and may be created as a result of the therapist's work with patient and mother. Oftentimes, the patient will have to get better in order to remove obstacles from the affective bond with the mother and, consequently, with the rest of the world, so that they can restore the affective balance at home.

We cannot expect that a mother who arrived at the hospital to admit her child after being attacked would be able to communicate what happened. I have heard mothers saying that the signs of aggression seen on their own bodies were but "caresses" of their children. Who could be sure of that? Nobody. It is only during treatment, following up with the mother, that we will be able to know whether there is a better way to show some love. An affective bond must be something rational, so there will be no destructive actions that, even at an unconscious level, could take homicidal proportions.

Creating an affective bond is something that depends on both the mother and the baby. Some babies reject their mothers at birth, and there is no normal mother who could ever react positively to that. If she is already affected in her narcissism, a pathologically narcissistic pair is created with a consequent filicide. *It takes two people to have a relationship*, and in this case it is the mother and the baby. The mother may have some pathological filicide and narcissism that, nevertheless, will only be triggered if the baby is genetically prone to contribute to it in her own (the baby's) future illness. Otherwise, she may be a normal baby and a happy adult.

I have addressed here a pathological, filicidal, and narcissistic relationship between baby and mother that remained "unresolved." Either one or both of them have ultimately shown an open case of psychosis with suicidal tendencies. Once again, I'd like to emphasize that I consider filicide to be *normal* in feeling and thought, as long as it is not effectively performed (acted upon) to become *pathological filicide*. *Normal* filicide and narcissism are the same as removing the obstructions to affective bond, both from the part of the mother and from the part of the child. It most often takes a therapist to facilitate the process.

Interrupting Treatment as a Pathological and Suicidal Filicide Conduct

Interrupting psychological treatment at the slightest indication that a child is improving is a common example of filicide at hospitals and outpatient facilities. I have already mentioned it, but it bears repeating. Throughout all these years of work at hospitals and outpatient facilities, I have observed and emphasized that it's harder for a father to allow his son to get well, as opposed to a daughter. That is why I always refer back to the "primitive hordes."

I had a patient whose father once said to me, in a very taxing way, "In my house there's only room for one man." To which I replied, "You should take very good care of yourself, because your son, despite being at risk of attempting suicide, has been treated with a lot of care so that he will not try to kill himself." A week later, the father died of a heart attack.

Overall, mothers don't have such a hard time seeing her child improving, whether it is a son or a daughter. However, when the issue is "lack of money"—which is almost always the alleged reason, mostly from fathers— mothers usually are in no position to argue and wind up agreeing with the husband. There's a tacit alliance between them to allow the son to remain ill (filicide) so that they can stay together, having the appearance of a couple.[41]

A few years ago I had the opportunity to notice the subtlety of a couple in the most sophisticated manifestation of unconscious filicide. When they noticed that their daughter had improved, the mother got terminal cancer and died. Then, the father discontinued the girl's college education and treatment. Unconsciously, he said to himself, "You got better and killed your mother, who had been unsuccessfully trying to kill you. This will cost you dearly. Now I'm the one who's going to kill you." And so he put an end to any possibility of her completing her treatment. Apparently, that was a case of matricide. However, those who had been studying the patient for many

---

41 This is the pathologically narcissistic couple I have mentioned before, in which each individual married himself or herself in the other. They look like a couple, but they are separated. As I wrote in *Psicoterapia do Paciente Psicótico*, they have not resolve their respective cases of pathological narcissism and are "each on their own corner." The ill child is the only link between the two of them.

years already knew that the mother had selected the worst possible therapists for her daughter. The girl became chronic and, when she finally got better, the mother died. In turn, the suicidal patient accepted that her treatment would be discontinued. She would rather use the money to buy new clothes.

Another case I mentioned before was that of a father who questioned the medication that was given to his daughter, telling me that I had to prescribe a medication that I knew would have many harmful side effects that, in the long-term, could become fatal. He started to put pressure on the daughter about her medication. Soon I realized I was irritated by it, but I was able to see right through him: He was trying to break the bond that we had created, after having such a hard time, by making things uncomfortable between me and the patient. That way, he (the father) would not have anything to do with the end of the treatment. I realized what he was doing in time to explain the situation to the patient.

Another interesting case is an example of how I treat this issue during a session with the patient. She was thirty two, single, a freelancer, and I treated her between 1980 and 1987. According to her, she had had unsuccessful treatments before, because she felt stuck at work and her love life. She couldn't pay for the treatment all by herself and needed some financial aid from her father, which really bothered her because it gave him the right to interfere and threaten putting an end to her treatment whenever they had a disagreement. This was the context when we had a session in October 1986, which I'll transcribe below.

Clinical Session

Carmem: Did your father talk to you about medication?

Patient: He did, and he wanted me to talk to you, too.

C: He wants to irritate me and push me away from you. This way, you won't get better, because I've seen this happen before and the story never ends well.

[She looks at me, so I continue.]

C: If I get irritated and you doubt me, I won't treat you my own way, giving you my all. You'll just be another patient, not my "number-one patient."[42] [The number one during her time slot, that is.]

P: Yeah? So...

C: Your father read *The Little Prince* and saw that he got very disappointed when he saw thousands of roses just like his. The fox had to tell him that his rose was special, because there was a connection between the two of them. Haven't you read *The Little Prince*?

P: I read it, but I didn't understand it. I thought it was a children's book. So what?

C: Your father was afraid of our connection.

P: What does it have to do with us?

C: He noticed that I see you as the Little Prince

---

42 "Patient #1" is seen as a total object and, as the only object of my observation and exchange of feelings at that moment.

sees his rose. [Special in her own time slot.]

P: Oh, I see it now. I was really second-guessing you and the medication. That is it. [She looks pensive.]

C: If I gave you the medication, you'd be in big trouble. You'd never trust me, right?

P: Yeah... But why does he want to do it?

C: Have you ever heard of filicide?

P: No. What is it?

C: Killing or mutilating a son or daughter, whether consciously or unconsciously. In your case, he wants to make you a chronic case, to mentally disable you. It is unconscious, as many cases I've seen before.

P: Son of a bitch! He always wanted to do that to me, with my friends, my boyfriends. I thought I was delusional.

C: You did?! [I stated.]

P: Why?

C: Because that way it would hurt less. [Had it been a delusion.]

P: Damn! I'm gonna kill this guy... And why does he do that to me, not to my sisters?

C: Because the other ones are "tamed crazies." They don't bother him, they don't make him think, "Oh, I have an hospitalized daughter." You're the one bothering him!

P: I'm the so-called "narcissism punching bag."

C: In the flesh. And he can't stand the relationship you have with me. And it's only by accident that it happened to me, because it could have been with any other therapist. He can't stand it because he can't have a bond with you. That's why he wants to put an end to your other relationships.

***

It was then that the patient felt her latent parricide, which is indeed taken into account in general treatment, maybe even treated as Oedipal material.

I also need to explain that, overall, mothers and fathers believe they have created their children's disease and feel impotent to make it disappear.[43] In treatment, medication and hospitalization constitute the only thing that they can perceive and discuss with the therapist.

The connection between therapist and patient, albeit as delicate and fragile as a spider's web, is invisible to the eyes of pathologically narcissistic parents[44], but their hearts are sensible to it. They feel that they are "losing" their child[45] when they see the patient getting better. They

_____

43 I have already described the subject in one of my books, entitled *Loucura: Mito e Realidade,* KBR, 2012.

44 As I mentioned before, pathological narcissism is different from normal narcissism. If it is pathological, each individual sees himself or herself in the other. In regular cases of narcissism, each individual sees the other in their own projective identifications. Therefore, they see others as they are indeed.

45 Actually, the child is not seen and experienced as such, but as a partial and local object, a placement for the projective identifications of the parents. As the child gets better, the parents' projective identifications return to themselves. They will have a true child, but must

can't understand that the next step is "winning" a normal child. However, we must not curse the unconscious filicide of parents once they react that way to their child's treatment due to fear of loss. Parents cannot understand that they won't lose their child with each improvement, not until therapists who have rid themselves of their own pathological narcissism tells them about the situation. And how can therapists do such a thing?

Above all, they cannot be irritated by "filicidal maneuvers" because we know that it's part of the growth of parents and patients—it's never a crime or a scandal. Then, they must be careful not to put patients against parents. Therapists must learn to deal with these and other feelings from parents and, in turn, with their own feelings. They need to be careful not to feed filicidal feelings towards their patients and, as I mentioned before, they must have overcome their own pathological narcissism; otherwise, therapists will take either the side of parents or that of patients, when their role is to actually be a mere spectator and explain the facts in an efficient way. Their emotional involvement would only stupefy them, obstructing the little understanding they could have of the "parents vs. patient" case.

As for the relationship between parents and therapists, I have already mentioned the most common issue with clinical practice: Medication. It is important to also emphasize the problems resulting from the need of hospi-

---

change themselves and withstand the suffering that comes with the changing process. It is not always possible, because some fathers and mothers wind up ill or die. These family structures are very firmly founded in their pathological narcissism.

talization for patients who are at risk of attempting suicide. At hospitals, it is common to discuss the risk of suicide, but pathologically narcissistic mothers and fathers—who believe they are great perfect parents—will hardly notice the possibility of their child committing suicide. For that to happen, they would need to see their child as a total object and, obviously, that is not the case if the child is admitted at the hospital. When parents fail to notice the risk of suicide, they usually move towards improperly and prematurely interrupting their child's treatment, who oftentimes end up killing themselves. That is when parents regret taking all warnings for granted.

Actually, each individual can only do their best and we, as therapists, must understand that. A patient's parents, whether they are normal or ill, have their limitations. Nobody is running for a demigod prize. Now, if therapists are well analyzed, they'll be humble enough to understand it and not be tempted to make accusations against the patient's parents.

This subject has already been addressed several times, but it's never too much to see it from other angles, since pathological filicide is something hard to be diagnosed and treated because it demands, as I already mentioned, that therapists admit that their own parents once wanted to kill them, whether consciously or unconsciously, and that they (the therapists) would then have responded with matricide or parricide feelings, whether consciously or unconsciously.[46] Few therapists enjoy

---

46 The feeling of filicide must be overcome in fantasy, not in concrete reality. The same is true for matricide, parricide, incest, fratricide, or suicide. If it does take place in reality, it results not only in psychosis,

treating themselves; few therapists are able to see themselves as "victims" or their parents as their "executioners" without becoming ill. In general, therapists analyze themselves without touching these issues, which are crucial to efficiently treat psychotic patients. These are a therapist's blind spot.

To conclude this section, it is good to remember that, in most parts, patients reach an agreement or decision to cut short their treatment. Through the suicidal will of an ill individual, we can clearly see the pathological filicide of the parents who refuse or interrupt the treatment of their child. On the other hand, as I always say, therapists cannot "fight" for the health of a patient when they're all on their own and the patient decides to offer his or herself as sacrifice in favor of the so-called union of his or her parents. When treating a patient who is at risk of suicide and whose treatment is interrupted, some people working with me already brace themselves before treatment is initiated by using the following document:

STATEMENT

I do hereby state that, for all due purposes, (patient's name) sought psychotherapeutic treatment with (therapist's name).

Considering the medical condition, a psychiatric evaluation was recommended.

The patient shows a condition compatible with

---

but in crime as well.

suicide attempts, according to the ICD. We must emphasize that the patient's life is still at risk and a new suicide attempt may take place at any time. We have also verified that the patient has difficulties handling the medication—sometimes the medication is not taken, sometimes it is interrupted, or taken at a different dose than that prescribed by the doctor. Considering the severity of the case and the fact that the patient's life remains at risk, it is our duty to inform parents and guardians about the condition, the risks involved, and the therapeutic proposal, in addition to request collaboration during the treatment and care demanded by the case.

The proposed treatment consists of the following:

1. *Psychiatric follow up, once a week, for patient evaluation and medication supervision.*
2. *Psychotherapy twice or three times a week, making it clear that the psychotherapist may request additional sessions if required.*
3. *Medication:*

   a. Antipsychotic and antiparkinsonian medication have been prescribed to help prevent side effects (such as permeation) and facilitate hypnosis.

   b. The medication must be kept by the parents and guardians, away from the patient, even though it is not lethal.

c. We request that parents be responsible for administering the medication at the times and doses prescribed, because the patient has proved to be incapable of doing it properly. Parents must also inform the therapist immediately in the event that the patient refuses to take the medication as prescribed.

4. *There will be a monthly meeting with the family, the patient, the psychotherapist, and the psychiatrist in order to evaluate treatment and guidelines and also verify the possibility of continuing treatment.*

5. *At the moment, hospitalization has not been indicated for the patient because there is a high risk of the case becoming chronic and the patient developing "hospitalism," a severe situation that may lead to loss of touch with reality, affection, and certain physical and intellectual abilities. However, the situation will be constantly monitored and, at a later time, a hospitalization period may or may not be necessary.*

6. *The proposal above is an attempt of treatment, but no guarantee is given in regards to results or the physical integrity of the patient. There is no time limit for the psychotherapeutic and psychiatric treatment as of now.*

Place and date

Individual in charge

Patient

Psychotherapist

Psychiatrist

On Therapists and Therapies

I must know that narcissists can only hear what comes from themselves.

Therapists must remember that the patient's mother had a mother from whom she received information, either good or bad, which can be helpful or not. And therapists must keep in mind that they have or had a mother too.[47] This way, they'll be able to separate facts regarding their patients, so as to not traumatize them with some comments, putting them against the mother.

Example: One of my patients didn't know how to identify what she was feeling. Despite the treatment, she felt worse every day. That was when I told her that it is only natural, that it is part of her process, because each day she starts to see herself as a person like all others, and maybe that is what is becoming unpleasant to her. The following account from a therapy session shows how I carried out her treatment.

---

47 Consequently, there must be a "well-resolved" relationship with the mother and the outside world so that patients can be treated properly.

Clinical Session

The session had already started and the patient complained about the lack of improvement, saying that everything was going badly. This was the dialog:

Carmem: Each day you get to know yourself better and realize you are a person like all others; maybe that's what's unpleasant to you.[48]

Patient: I agree. I thought I was better than others, and now I see I'm worse. My head is spinning.

C: Spinning or in doubt?

P: [Excited] Finally someone understands me! I'm always in doubt[49] and life is like hell. There's always a fight inside of me. [She pumps one fist against the other] I wish someone could tell me why.

I get some paper and a pen and draw a road for her. On one side of the road, I wrote "Yes" and, on the opposite side, I wrote "No." At the end of the road, right in the middle, I wrote "Perhaps." I tell her that so far, while being guided by me, she had gone down her road in the YES/NO direction, redoing things she should have done

---

48 I have explored the subject in my book *Psicoterapia do Paciente Psicótico, op. cit.*

49 Actually, it was not a matter of clear, honest "doubt." There were millions of doubts regarding everything and everybody, which brought her confusion and despair.

when she was a baby, being led by her mother, in order to reach "Perhaps." Throughout her life, she had never been able to resolve "Perhaps" by herself in time to avoid so many years of suffering.

> P: That's it! [She's ecstatic] My Mom could never really do it. Wanna know why? Because every time the "grownups" in our village would get together they never knew if they could, for example, rearrange a piece of furniture because they weren't familiar with Brazilian laws. [The patient was a descendent of foreigners living in Brazil.]

In spite of all her suffering, this patient was able to have a nice life and never had to be admitted. She's a successful business owner. She still suffers because she's facing doubts about herself and everybody who surround her. But now they are indeed *doubts*. She has to double-check everything, withstand depressive moments, and times of pain, despite the fact that she has seen a fantastic improvement in only two years, two sessions a week, sometimes longer than fifty-minutes each. I never prescribed anything to her, so nobody would ask, "Does she require hospitalization?" In this patient's story, her filicide was resolved in a pathological way, because her mother had been the victim of the same problem.[50]

Apparently, she was what we would call neurot-

---

50 The mother, in turn, didn't have a mother with a sufficiently structured ego to indicate the "yes" and "no" paths.

ic, and she was attending psychotherapy sessions. Actually, she was somehow experiencing depressive moments thanks to the new work on forming her normal ego as an adult person. In her case, her ego had developed prematurely, without strong defenses, as Winnicott says. But I can't leave aside the work that I do on her basic pathological narcissism, the filicide she suffered from, and the need to always second guess everything that crosses her mind, and discuss everything with me—according to her, I'm her "only interlocutor" (sic). I tell her that a little bit of suspicion is always good; otherwise, she would be at the mercy of everything and everybody, as well as of her emotions and urges. She needs to talk to me so that she can reach her own conclusions.

P: I have doubts about you.

C: It is very important that you're able to tell someone that you don't trust them. It's an important step towards the formation of your ego and your emotional growth. Telling me that you don't trust me is a start for you to trust me. If you didn't have any trust at all, you wouldn't even come to my office.

Anyway, in this case the most important thing is that she was using her most primitive defenses (projective identifications, disassociation, introjection, repression) [51]

---

[51] Personally, I believe repression comes necessarily along projective and introjective identification. If there weren't a primitive repression, there wouldn't be disassociation.

and finally building a true ego. I know I'm of no importance to her; I'm nothing but a catalyst. She says it herself sometimes, "Just pretend it's happening to you. But it
isn't. It's just a way for you to understand me better." Even
though she is really ill, she's afraid of hurting me. I'm the
only person she can count on, because she believes I give
her "emotional space" (holding) so that she can tell me
what she thinks with such difficulty and pain.

It is important that I *make believe*—she says "It's
not really about you," but I must "pretend" that she's okay
with me, that the anger is outside. We both knew it was a
lie, but she couldn't stand being told that at the moment. It
would be a filicide attempt, that is, her treatment would be
interrupted, because she would choose to do so. Her ego
will only be strong enough to hear that later on, when it's
no longer necessary that I tell her things, because she will
be telling them to herself. She is also angry at me because
she wanted to have been cured already, but I can't tell her
that because, to her, I still don't exist and my words would
sound absurd.[52]

The fact that I stated that she needed a little suspicion in her life does not mean that I was feeding a severe
psychotic symptom, but a very useful *defense* mechanism
for the paranoid schizophrenia phase. As I understood
from Winnicott, a premature ego is incapable of paranoia,
because it had to form itself very quickly by building a

52 This is one of the most common things patients say after several
years of psychoanalysis: "I know what Dr. So and So said was right, but
he didn't even get close to the issue." I don't think it's just a problem
with timing during the interpretation, but the need to, first of all, help
patients have an ego, *so that they can reach a conclusion by themselves*

false self. Therefore, it cannot move from the paranoid schizophrenia phase—and experience that abundance of defenses that arise throughout the emotional development process—to the depressive phase, in which objects are seen as total objects. In a premature ego, fragility is a constant and the false self that had been built crumbles at the slightest sign of contradiction or a deeper frustration.

On the subject of a false *self*, I intend to develop something in another opportunity, since I see patients in my own office and, oftentimes, they have this severe problem associated with a deficient creativity that has mostly been fertilized by inadequate treatment. I'd like to point out the fact that, if psychotherapists and psychoanalysts work on their own false self, they unfortunately develop a filicidal action towards the patient, because they are unaware of their own filicide, which could have opportunely been identified, treated, and overcome.

By the way, it is extremely difficult and painful to have your ego built or rebuilt during a psychotherapy or psychoanalytical treatment. Patients often abandon or interrupt treatment when they need their therapist the most. They frequently don't have the courage to tell therapists what they feel about them and, in order to not spoil the "wonderful relationship" they have already created, patients decide to interrupt treatment. There are cases when therapists themselves "discharge" patients.

Having a false self doesn't mean that it is impossible to live a satisfactory life forever. The concern is that these people have had a "rupture" due to the false self, and that is why they had to seek treatment.

Going back to what I think about pathological

narcissism, I recommend that we don't try to work with transferences because, as the name itself indicates, this pathology refers to Narcissus' self-absorption. *These patients are alone; they don't have an external object to which they can direct their affection.* In order to have these patients objectify their libido, a therapist must go around their pathological narcissism and, once it is cured, they can think of transference or, better yet, directing their libido towards the therapist and then *from one person to another* in a concrete way.

I remember this patient who heard from her analyst that she (the patient) wanted to kill herself because she was mad at him (the therapist). The answer was brief, but effective: "If I had the ability to *be mad at somebody*, do you really think I would kill myself? But this incoherent and stupid interpretation has just allowed me to be mad at you and now I think I won't kill myself anymore." In this case, the patient's pathological narcissism prevailed, which makes us think that maybe the analyst resorted to this fortunate maneuver intentionally. The patient can't put up with stupid people; she felt narcissistically attacked and opened a "door of understanding" for the therapist when she was enraged by the "stupid interpretation." Upon verifying that, at the height of her "wisdom," she had selected a stupid analyst, she stepped outside herself to turn to the outside world. This patient was someone special and, despite being a lunatic, she always spoke her mind and was able to cure herself.

Timing is an important part of treatment; that is, the moment when we can touch such a delicate and painful subject as filicide. Patients need to be ready to hear the therapist, who should never use an accusatory tone, just a functional and informative one. And that is why therapists must be well-resolved individuals as far as their own pathological narcissism and filicide are concerned.

In outpatient facilities, patients have already been subjected to therapy and, consequently, are more integrated, so it's easier to touch the subject. Still, we must make sure that we know these patients so we can anticipate their possible reactions. Patients who are hospitalized need extra care, because they can get into action despite hospital protection. Experiencing concrete thought before such a revelation—"Your parents unconsciously wish you dead"—, patients may either have an argument with their parents or attack the therapist. Some may even attempt suicide. You can never be too careful with such a revelation, which exposes psychotic patients to something similar to a tumor in their psychological life, which needs to be exposed and treated.

A good example of how to approach a psychotic is the case of a patient of mine who used to put his mother on a pedestal. However, she was very ill and hadn't given him any assistance. She passed away. Today, the son is a chronic patient. I cannot turn to him and say, "Your mother was in no condition of liking you, because she didn't like herself." That patient would raise up against it and maybe even abandon treatment.

While having a fit against her, he would say, "Mommy had this thing that she would always worry about me, but look at me now! It was no use!" But I couldn't tell him, "It's good that you're angry at your mother. She really was in no emotional state to take care of you and you have the right to be mad at her." This surreptitious clarification could, little by little, become deeper as he realizes that it is no blasphemy to be mad at the mother of whom he took so much care, but who could never care for him. There will come a time when he'll be able to hear that his mother, unconsciously, desired his death just as much as he can desire hers now. That is no manifestation of illness; it's a manifestation of health.

Therefore, treating filicide and its consequences, along with pathological narcissism, must be done with extreme care. *We must take into account who is doing the talk (the therapist), the state of a patient who is listening, and the timing and tone in which things are being said.* As far as therapists, some are in no condition to meet the requirements and treat something so difficult as pathological narcissism. In such case, they had better give up this task, under the penalty of witnessing a tragedy. However, many therapists have already resolved their own issues even before they work on individual analysis, and that is why they are not shocked or astonished with possible references to such facts.

There was this time when a patient told me that, when he was a teenager, he often thought about how his parents should die, but never felt any remorse for thinking that way. [This family had a good holding environment for such feelings to be expressed.] He asked me if that was very severe. To that, I replied that it was just the opposite—a very healthy thought. It meant that his parents had only thought about filicide, but never acted upon it. Upon channeling such feelings, he reacted by thinking that they should die too. This patient got along just fine with his parents and, when they died, he went through mourning normally, as Grinberg would say.

I consider it to be pathological when someone's narcissism hardly allows the individual to receive ideas or feelings from the outside, from external objects. That's what happens, for example, with some very severe patients who are hospitalized, become encysted, and are then truly inaccessible, unreachable. They will hardly be cured, no matter how much the hospital team tries to reach out to them, because nothing will do.

Other patients, such as drug addicts, are even less reachable, because they don't even have an ego that can be disassembled and only express themselves in delusional ideas or hallucinations. These are people who have mostly stopped developing during their autoerotic phase and are *acting out* their "feelings" in their own bodies. They cannot resolve any of their emotions at the mental level, and if they do, it's only very little of it.

So, let's take an alcoholic, for example, who instead of *thinking* in suicide will *kill himself little by little*, starting with the liver. He says that he'll never drink again. At the first sign of distress, he goes back to the bottle. A cocaine addict says he uses the drug because he "likes it" and he could give it up at any time. That's untrue. He knows he can have a cardiac arrest and die after consuming any amount of the drug, but he feels superior to the rest of humanity. He is immortal.

Consequently, treating these patients becomes harder than treating a schizophrenic. Actually, you just need to ask Alcoholics Anonymous, which provides patients with a holding environment that we, therapists, are unable to. It's a shame that it's so hard to make someone seek the help of the AA.

Therapy is actually a *dialog*[53,] as long as therapists knows that they are on the patient's side, working with their affection, and a little bit with their thoughts and behaviors. Above all, they need the patient to feel them. When something *new* comes from a patient, therapists are often caught off guard and, in case therapists are strictly following their theories and cannot be themselves, they won't know how to act. A case comes to mind, and it involved a very aggressive female patient. After a given interpretation, the therapist was expecting a slap the face, but was surprised with a kiss. The therapist didn't understand what was going on—and nor should the therapist understand it; she was supposed to only feel it. However, let's not imagine that at psychotic patient is able to understand *interpretations*. The dialog must be simple, based on what's *real*, on subjects related to the daily life at the hospital or the routine of outpatients, on facts that are reported by patients and/or their families.

---

53 Exchanging true experiences, so that patients will feel comfortable to share their dreams, feelings, and thoughts. I believe the ideal therapist is the one who once had schizophrenia and is now cured, just as people in the Alcoholics Anonymous can help other alcoholics, since they can truly understand them.

How does a psychotic patient understand interpretations?

Psychotic patients understand and feel the interpretation as an *attack* because, in general, their thinking is concrete. That's why they either abandon treatment, or retaliate against the therapist either physically or by attacking his/her narcissism. I usually call it a "monologue of two."

As far as therapists go, I'll say it once again: in the event that therapists themselves have pathological narcissism, it would represent a serious threat to the treatment of a psychotic patient. Without adequate emotional conditions, they would feel attacked by either a patient's improvement or by the explicit aggression. Therefore, first of all, therapists must first subject themselves to an efficient treatment.

The Issue With Truth in Therapy

During therapy, there is the issue of how both the therapist and the patient will deal with the *truth*. One or the other may feel affected by a word said the wrong way or a feeling that wasn't expressed well. Basically, it's an echo of pathological narcissism. Therapists must abandon their neutral position and the presumption that they know something about the patient. They may know a lot about the patient, but it's always *knowledge of the outside— the patient's exterior shell—,* and much more effort will be required to touch the heart of the patient, his or her true state. That is why an efficient dialog will be reached.

Bion tells us that we must work without memory or desire. In the case of patients who are in the process of or have already become chronic, we must act as their *memory* and share their *desire* to improve.[54]

The Issue With Time vs. Space

As we know, the unconscious mind is atemporal and, consequently, many severe patients are really distressed until they can become aware of their surroundings, both as a matter of time and space, because things come to their mind out of order. Paradoxically, they need it "not to become insane" (sic). Organizing something that has no structure is an attempt to structure their *ego* a little bit. That is why it is of great help to know a patient's true (real) history of patients by keeping in touch with their family, both at a hospital and an outpatient setting. This history is what will tell us how and where there was a failure to form and develop their ego, when and where patients suffered the first interruption in their develop-

---

54 I have a female patient who subjected herself to so many electroshock therapy sessions that she has lost her memory. I am her memory and, little by little, she can resolve her "time vs. space" issue with the real information I provide to her. As a matter of fact, I've known her for many, many years, so I can actually do that. Under other circumstances, I would only be able to help patients rebuild their memories from information provided by family members and other individuals.

ment. It's easier with outpatients, because in general they provide the information to therapists. Now, with severely psychotic individuals, we need more help from the family because they'll hardly collaborate with information because they either fear being considered a very severe case, or because of trust issues, or because they've had memory lapses.

The contact between therapists and their asylum patients is crucial. It is with daily follow-up that therapists can observe the results of what was said during a therapy session, of how it was perceived. Ultimately, therapists will see how effective the treatment has been, so that they can either modify or continue with the same technique.

Here's an example: A patient got mad at me when I told her that she shouldn't insist on using the computer, which frustrates her so much. She should take a stroll or do something else to fill the void left by her frustration of not being able to write as well as she narcissistically thought she could. I don't acknowledge that I have noticed her anger. She had already been very hurt by herself, affected in her *narcissistic wound* known as *inaptitude*, for me to have a word or sentence to take her away from true pain.

Would it be right for me to say, "Are you angry at me because I'm pointing out your difficulty in hearing me, or your difficulty in writing as brilliantly as you imagined you could?" She would turn her affection towards me, instead of listening to what she really needs to do, which is being in touch with herself to verify that she is unhappy with her performance.

On the following session, she told me exactly what

I refrained from uttering: She was disappointed in herself. Then I could add that, despite of everything, she was able to hear my suggestion. That's when she felt happy and told me that she organized a choir group with other patients, which was really good for her—she allowed herself to let her hair down a little bit. I asked her if she had been mad at me. She says that she had, but finally understood that she shouldn't demand so much of herself.

I'm not trying to say that all chronic patients easily respond to a therapist's intervention. For some patients, the destruction of their affection, thoughts, and memory—either perpetrated by themselves or by others—was so deep, with such severe repercussions in their behavior, that it became almost impossible to treat them, especially in a short period of time. The example I had given was of that patient who is twenty seven and has been ill for fifteen years, but was able to go to college for two years.

Another patient, whom I've been treating for twenty one years, hasn't had the same performance and is a true challenge to me. I met her at a clinic, coming from a treatment with about five hundred electroshocks, insulin shock therapy, and Cardiazol treatment. She could barely say a word here and there. She couldn't even think. She expressed herself through her conduct by attempting suicide all the time. She would ingest the first thing that she'd see in front of her: soap, any type of liquid, pencils, kitchen knives, and whatever else she could get her hands on. She would break the entire clinic once a week and physically assault the psychiatric aide to the point that she broke someone's nose. Nobody would dare get near her. She was part of an analysis group to which I administered medication. This treatment lasted about three years and, unfortunately, it was interrupted. She had already started forming thoughts and expressing feelings with words, but she was referred to individual analysis and taken home by a group of psychiatric aides.

I left that clinic, but never lost sight of her. She would call me in the middle of the night to invite me for "a little whiskey." I'd then ask her to go wake up the nurse— who should be up anyway if he were aware of how severe the patient's situation was—and then recommended that he took care of the patient. Later, when she went looking for me at the "Margaridas" Protected Hostel (it was mid-1979), she had psychoanalysis sessions with a renowned colleague of mine. That was when, bit by bit, I started to realize that there was something wrong. From the time I was eighteen years old and working at the Pinel Clinic in Porto Alegre, I had seen a large number of psychotic patients who abandoned treatment. Statistically, the problem was not the patients, but the method or technique being implemented. My hypothesis then surfaced, which is now a certainty corroborated by my study of Bion's work: You can make patients become chronic by interpreting what they say as if the material was provided from a depressive position, when it actually comes from a paranoid schizophrenia stage.

I'll emphasize this concept by referring to the same patient. I was forced to interrupt the psychoanalysis sessions she was having with my renowned colleague when I told the patient's mother that she could no longer remain at the "Margaridas" Protected Hostel due to her aggressive conduct. Actually, while unable to express herself through language, the patient had regressed and adopted an extremely destructive conduct.

At the request of her mother, I started to treat her at my office. On the very first day, she repeated what she had done with the previous psychoanalyst. She would call me dishonest and try to leave the room before the session was over. I did not allow her to by holding her and locking the door. Then, for the remaining forty nine minutes of our session, I told her who was the dishonest one between the two of us, since I had been following her case since the beginning of her illness and had become her memory. At the end of the session, when I gave her all the adjectives that her aggressive conduct suggested, she calmly made one request: "Can we go on for a few minutes longer?" This patient needed boundaries that the *"psychoanalytical setting"* could only provide in very rare exceptions. She was sure that in my office she would get the care that she needed for the time being. To this day, she still allows me to observe when the *new* arises of her and, as a therapist, I always stay [55]one step behind her, at least, to anticipate a risk of suicide, for example, so that I can admit her to a hospital if needed without feeling discredited by doing so.

I am relieved when I notice that she's getting worse. There was this time when, in the middle of a session, she was the one who told me that, "Galileo and some people of his time suffered so much for thinking and, this way, they truly lived their lives." I asked her if she was referring to herself as well. She told me that she did suffer a

---

55 It is not about physically putting yourself behind someone, but being aware that I come from the perspective of someone who knows even less about these patients than they know themselves.

great deal, saying that "My fantasies have gone away, even though I still see a few souls once in a while." She was referring to the delusional ideas and hallucinations she once had, but had no need for any longer. However, as everybody who experiences it, she missed her "fantasies."

I've learned a lot from her, such as the importance of the notion of space vs. time when treating psychosis, and the need to be therapist and patient at the same time in order to reach the ill individual. I'll explain: If I can't listen to the ill individual as the patient that I am—referring to my ill side—, I won't be able to understand her. I will be entrenched in my own head, hidden in my "neutrality"—some colleagues of mine still do that—and push away any understanding that goes through me and the other. For me to be able to treat a narcissistic patient, I must first look at myself in the mirror, as the mythical Narcissus once did. However, I have no obligation to commit suicide. I have to recognize myself as a *total object* in order to see my patients as a Total Object.

In sum, I'd like to introduce the code of good therapists treating psychotic individuals:

a. Playing the role of new and efficient mother, treating first the basic feelings of pathological narcissism and filicide, so that you can establish a relationship with your patient as a total object, not a projection of yourself.

b. As a new mother, creating an "*adequate holding*," that is, an affectionate environment for the patient's feelings and conduct, offering them understanding, but also setting boundaries, which is a crucial condition to restructure their ego or even to form a new ego.

c. As a good mother-therapist, being psychologically available, that is, effectively listening to the patient without pigeonholing them according to theories. Trying to feel what they feel. Trying to explain their conduct or feelings, whether you've understood what they reveal, or confessing them the truth otherwise.

d. Ridding yourself of vanity. Leaving room for patients, *the only person who is important to themselves, as therapists are important to themselves*, as I have written in *Psicoterapia do Paciente Psicótico*.

e. Always keeping in mind that psychotic individuals only perform a minimum transference; they are incapable of elaborating what they're told in a symbolic way. Therefore, their transference relationship with the therapist is a fictional one, as well as their relationship with anyone else in the outside world.

f. Seeking treatment with a therapist who has, at least, gone through personal psychoanalysis, or with a psychoanalyst.

g. Being convinced that, if patients need it, they should be medicated or hospitalized, even though the approach may be contrary to their convictions as a therapist, because the only thing that matters is these patients and their need to be understood while suffering, to get help when they need someone to take charge and prevent their chronic state or suicide.

h. Keeping in mind that suicide exists and

there's no use denying it—certain theories suggest that mental illnesses shouldn't even be acknowledged.

i. Remaining available to patients and their families to help them during emergencies. Keeping constant touch with the family or a relative, whether the patient is hospitalized or not.

j. Being careful not to use patients as targets for your own projections.

k. Not creating a paranoid couple with the patient by refraining to use information that comes from the outside (family members), thus avoiding that the treatment be discontinued by the patient or the family.

l. Observing your limitations at work, since you're not a universal therapist.

m. Speak up if you have been affected by aggressive acts committed against you, so as to avoid repeating the passive attitude of a pathologically narcissistic mother.

n. Seeking supervision whenever you have questions regarding the progress of a patient's treatment.

Considering everything that has been addressed in this chapter, it is clear that you cannot resort to the so-called *neutrality* of psychoanalysts when dealing with psychotic patients. These subjects have been developed in detail in my book *Psicoterapia do Paciente Psicótico*.

Symbiosis and Narcissism[56]

Within the scope of the mind, symbiosis[57] takes place when two beings live merely emotionally as one, and it is one of the expressions of pathological narcissism. It is a state that deserves careful analysis, because its comprehension comes as a result of successfully treating important mental illnesses.

It is obvious that symbiosis arises of the mother-and-baby relationship; it is the perfect physical and emotional connection that takes place in utero and is clearly indicated by the existence of an umbilical cord.

As the name suggests, symbiosis entails the fixation of a child in a very primitive stage of emotional development and, concomitantly, the behavior of a mother during and, above all, after the gestational period, when the pathological narcissism of psychotic personalities become concrete, whether or not they present a psychosis.

---

56 Based on Chapter 3 of *Psicoterapia do Paciente Psicótico*.
57 Symbiosis in Greek means "common life, intimacy." In Biology, it represents a long-term association that is mutually beneficial to two or more beings, such as lichens, which are the result of an intimate association between an algae and a fungus.

However, not all pathological narcissists express their narcissism through symbiosis. Some are able to overcome the issue; others contain it at least at the "mental" level.

Considering all the knowledge we have nowadays, mother and child are a single individual, despite being two people during pregnancy. At the beginning—let's say, during the first month—the mother is still normal and does not realize the existence of a child in her womb, even though she can imagine how the baby is in such stage and how she will be once she's born. As the months go by, she not only imagines it, but also feels the child inside of her and will then start to live with it. She got used to the life as a couple, in such a way that she acts and reacts as if she and the baby were *one single person*, even during birth, when there is separation and it becomes clear that there had always been two different people from the very beginning.

The birth is a very important and decisive moment, both for the mother and for the baby. There may be postpartum depression in normal women and episodes of psychosis in psychotic (pathologically narcissistic) individuals, for whom realizing that they're losing a part of themselves is emphasized more than the fact that they have welcomed a child. This psychotic rupture, as felt by the mother, always brings some kind of change, at different levels, in the deeply symbiotic relationship that mother and child have been keeping both physically and mentally.

Mothers who have not overcome their pathologically narcissistic phase are unable to perceive or realize the concrete separation from the child at birth. They continue to act as if they had been carrying the child in their womb, as if both were one single person. Many mothers do not have a sufficiently strong ego to develop a psychotic crisis, not even to have a small subclinical crisis that, overall, goes unnoticed. They couldn't even suffer a true episode of postpartum psychosis, in which they would acutely and concretely feel their disconnection from the child.

I believe that the emotional maintenance of a symbiotic situation depends in great part on the expectant mother's ability to suffer separation during birth. This ability is manifested in small psychotic crises a few days after birth, such as excitement and difficulty sleeping, or crying episodes without apparent reason. I'd go as far as saying that it is in and through these small manic and depressive crises that the rupture becomes effective, since the mother is able to feel and suffer what is indeed a loss, not only of a part of herself, but also of a physical and mental state. She shows that she's able to reorganize her life once again as an independent being.

Postpartum psychotic episodes are very diversified. I don't believe it is necessary to line them all up. What I wish to make very clear here is that these crises reveal a very favorable situation for the newborn, allowing her excellent conditions for emotional development with the unconscious certainty that the mother has effectively ruptured the symbiotic situation, thus releasing the child for a future complete independence.

A mother who is unable to mentally break the symbiotic connection at birth will always keep her child dependent on her, while she also depends on such dependence. This explains how difficult it is to have an eventual treatment that involved both mother and child.

It could happen that, in a case of emotional symbiosis, the mother gets pregnant again. Then the symbiotic pair is broken. The mother is free, whole, and available to a second symbiotic state. The child then abruptly feels mutilated, feeling only *one half*, as she indeed is. She may become ill or her symptoms are aggravated. "She got sick when her mother got pregnant with the second child." In fact, the rupture of such a situation is very critic, in that there are internal objects missing and the person becomes an extension of the mother, who is a concrete external object. The removal of this support acts as a death sentence due to the inability that it has brought to the child, since birth, of reorganizing her mental life. That is how entire psychotic families are created.

Understanding the continuity of a symbiotic state between mother-and-baby is crucial for therapists. If you can detect the symbiotic origins of a mental illness, you'll understand that, despite being an independent individual with all adequate requirements—the vital organs and systems needed to have a life of their own—, a patient may have never been born and remain a *nobody* for a pathologically narcissistic mother. In regards to the mother, if she doesn't even have enough room inside for her own parental objects, how could she be able to objectify the image of her own child? That child will always be a concrete part of her body. The only thing that actually exists is herself and her vital needs. It's as if there were two bodies and one single mind, her mind, in a concretized figuration. The child is only a physical and "mental" attachment to her own body.

The mother of a teenage boy hospitalized at the "Margaridas" Protected Hostel always comes to mind,[58] because she had an acute psychosis crisis. Her crisis represented an improvement in their symbiotic state, because going mad requires a certain degree of mental health. The mother then felt lost, confused with the individual act of the son, but still hospitalized him by fearing a possible physical aggression. Would a pseudopodium turning against the rest of the body be an unconceivable scene for a symbiotic, narcissistic individual?

"How come a part of myself wants to become independent of me?" That is the unconscious question that this mother asks, even though she cannot do anything while she is also experiencing the situation of interdependence with her child. This patient of mine at "Margaridas" recovered within a week (masochism?) and the mother "requested" that he came back home immediately. She said, "I don't care if he's healthy or ill, whether or not he needs treatment—the only thing that matters is that I need him, that's all!"

I believe that what happened to the two of them—or the *one* both represented, if we take into account their deep symbiotic situation—was that the son had a psychotic crisis and showed that he was healthy and alive in an attempt, despite belated, of becoming independent, even though it would only be at the physical level. That doesn't mean that he was able to mentally disconnect from her, so much so that he had another crisis and no longer can use

58 The "Margaridas" Hostel was founded in 1973, as already described in my book *Personalidade Psicótica e Psicose*. It was the first "Protected Hostel" in Brazil.

his health.

I will explain myself better: The psychotic crisis of this teenager was a healthy one, because it was only an attempt to separate himself from his mother. However, it was followed by an ill crisis, because he didn't know what to do with his new-found independence, since he hadn't been "mentally" fit to become independent. He used the little bit of independence that he had in the first place, which was his own health, to attack his mother in a manifestation of his illness. And he was hospitalized as a "mad" young men, because at a certain point in time he was unable to contain himself.

While he was living symbiotically with his mother, as "one half," everything was okay. But when he suddenly tried to act independently, he unconsciously realized that he was living as "one half" and was able to have a psychotic crisis, which I consider a healthy one. The mother also started to feel as only "one half" and could barely stand that fact, because the rupture in their unconscious agreement had been too abrupt, without the preparation she needed. Had this mother been able to make (create) projective identifications, she would have had a psychotic crisis as well, thus destroying the symbiosis and allowing her son to be himself.

This symbiosis obstructs, or does not foster the formation of projective identifications, since each time one of the components of the symbiotic pair tries to have a projective identification, he or she may be projecting a part of him or herself in the other. [59] *That is opposite to a baby, who can*

---

59 The Other as a concrete extension of himself or herself.

have projective identifications in the mother as someone
living outside herself and physically disconnected from her.

In the case of the symbiotic pair, the baby experiences the mother and vice-versa, while both are a physical extension of one another. Each one internally lives uncomfortably as a "non-being," which doesn't bother them as much as a psychotic crisis, which is the attempt of undoing a symbiotic and pathologically narcissistic bond. If, on the one hand, the symbiotic situation doesn't bother them as much, on the other hand it offers the exits that a psychotic crisis can foster. I'm more convinced each day that there is no such thing as a symbiotic patient, but a symbiotic, pathologically narcissistic pair—mother and child—that in terms of treatment must be considered as a set, as *one single person*. For each one of them, mother and child, to be individualized, this primitive person *"mother-and-baby"* must die (psychologically, of course.) Not all components of this pair can stand this necessary "death" for them to be effectively born as independent individuals. If the mother does not receive therapeutic treatment concomitantly, the child's treatment is prone to fail.

A few paragraphs above, I mentioned the potentially masochist behavior of the teenager in question. It is just that someone less prone to annihilation, to the state of "non-being," would have taken longer to heal from a psychotic crisis, thus providing the mother—his other half—more time for her to also gather herself after the symbiotic situation was broken. Therefore, this mother could even remain very psychotically ill, but she would have broken away from the sick experience of being "one half" while still looking like a complete person. A longer time triggered by the teenager's crisis would have granted her the ability to overcome the "birth" of her son, albeit belated, so that she could finally reclaim her own independence as an individual as well. Upon improving little by little, I would say that my patient actually got worse. He thought he was immediately ready to reestablish the symbiotic connection, which goes unnoticed by laypersons but we therapists know to be extremely destructive for both mother and child. Therefore, upon observing the facts, I came to the conclusion that my patient's brief cure from a psychotic crisis was a manifestation of masochism, or rather "suicide" would be a better word to designate his return to a state of "non-being."

In these cases of symbiotic existence, we also need to understand the behavior of a mother who tries to interrupt the treatment of her hospitalized child. Once she is separated from him, she suddenly and abruptly sees herself at the mercy of her self-destructive internal urges. Once her other half is missing, she needs to "recover" that other part of herself, the child. On the other hand, her inability to internalize images and the fact that she cannot see her child, she cannot have him near her, leads her to the unpleasant feeling that he no longer exists. She then starts to seriously fantasize about his death. The life threat that she feels towards herself is also a very violent one.

Therefore, we can understand that she does not remove her son from his hospital treatment because she's mean. It is purely a symbiotic, pathological narcissism issue that is heavier on its symbiosis than in its narcissism. In a relationship in which the symbiosis had been undone, even though mother and child were pathologically narcissistic individuals, it is highly unlikely that the mother would interfere in the patient's treatment.

Considering the above, we can conclude that assisting the family is crucial to the success of a patient's treatment. Observing the parent's behavior and, above all, the behavior of a mother to psychotic patients, I have been able to understand the creation and structuring of a psychotic family. Today, I'd also add that filicide is in the foundations of a symbiotic situation: A son who is not even born as an individual and remains an appendix of an extremely ill mother.

Filicide: A Constant in Human History

These notes and considerations are not intended to be an exhaustive exploration of the subject matter. They are only intended to prove that pathological filicide exists and is present since the most remote ages, being recorded in History, Religions, Literature, and through several cultural manifestations without causing major controversy.

In Greece, the cradle of Western culture, the practice of eliminating children was part of their custom. Parents used to choose the children who should survive, mainly preferring boys over girls, for they would be future warriors. Female children were more easily sacrificed. As a cultural expression, I don't believe we can consider it pathology in the part of their parents.

The same used to happen in Ancient Rome, where the yet current Roman Laws were created. Children were also sacrificed there and, right after babies were born, the father would decide whether he or she should live. Some were saved by their mothers, who would deliver them to a servant or slave to raise. We must keep in mind that, in their private life, Romans did not obey the Civil Laws they had created themselves.

Filicidal practices have not decreased throughout the centuries and are more notorious in the Middle Ages. We know that during the Crusades—which are not as closely related to religion as we first thought, but primarily economy-driven—kings would send their sons (*infantes*) to the war, thus sacrificing them for acquisitions and profits. The same happened later, when new lands were discovered and monarchs would send their children to rule them, thus severely risking their lives in lands that were frequently inhospitable.

In more modern times, pathological filicide is perpetrated by Heads of State who order wars from their offices, where their own children go to fight and make parents proud. I believe they are conceited, but they may be simply following the destiny of humanity phylogenetically: The father is the only one who owns the properties of the tribe, the women, and homes, while sons must be punished for an eventual rebellion.

In current times, filicide remains alive. The Vietnam War is an example, since the United States wanted to "save" the Asian nation from the "Communist terror." Many atrocities have been committed, not only against the Vietnamese people, but against young Americans as well, who rebelled against a war that was not theirs to fight.

They were all severely punished by their homeland. Some went into self-imposed exile and left the country; others went to prison as deserters. There are those who died in battle; others returned home mutilated and addicted to drugs, usually becoming criminals in violent vengeful episodes against society, in mass murders in plain daylight. It was payback time with parricide, matricide, and filicide.

That goes without mentioning all those who committed suicide in Vietnam by overdosing, or are still killing themselves to this date in the United States, following the intentions of their generals (parents) who "ordered" their death. Also in the 20th century, Hitler satisfied his pathological narcissism and, in addition to the genocide of people of Jewish and other origins—mainly Russians—he sacrificed teenage Germans after he had run out of boots on the ground, sending them to fight a war he knew he had already lost.

What calls our attention is that, throughout History, this type of pathological suicide always has fathers and sons as protagonists. It seems to prove the compulsive need to repeat the behavior of savage hordes, in which father and son fight for the ownership of females within the group. We have also noticed that, as Oedipus, the death initiative comes from the father. Then, the son fights back.

In Brazil, a unique kind of genocide has been observed since 1964: Fathers are unemployed heads of the family and thousands of children live and die in hunger due to the mismanagement of public funds that are wasted with construction projects—some of them too luxurious, others unnecessary and abandoned when they are half-way done—, not to mention the recent millions of dollars that have been stolen from the Federal Budget. You can also add to this list the mass sterilization of poor women who seek Social Welfare services when they are in labor. Genocide is filicide. The homeland is killing their own children.[60]

In regards to genocide and filicide in Brazil, there is still a serious problem with children who are abandoned. They are known as "children of the streets," a concept that some people use only to promote themselves or capitalize on it. Large sums of money are earmarked for governmental institutions to take care of destitute children, but these funds wind up rerouted or used poorly. Denouncing the death of children from destitute families is never enough. They either die due to poor services available at hospitals or a lack of basic sanitation. It is the Motherland killing her children, oftentimes even before they are able to go to school, that is, if there are schools available nearby.

We don't need to travel back in time or even leave the house to meet Hitler. Genocide happens here in Brazil, and it is more intense each day. How come people go to bed hungry and die of hunger in a country like this? How many (1-10) benefit from this killing without even paying for the funeral? The AIDS epidemic is another sad case of pathological filicide. Funds are sent from other countries for AIDS treatment, but it never reaches the sick.[61]

In the form of fiction, literature gives us many examples of pathological filicide, some more explicit than others. Among children's stories, "Snow White and the Seven Dwarves" is a reproduction of the Oedipus

---

60 Editor's note: The original text was written in 1992, but astonishingly the history of government corruption keeps repeating itself, even though child mortality rates have decreased.

61 The information on funds for AIDS treatment date from 1992.

Myth. Oedipus' biological parents ordered his death. The Step-Mother Queen ordered the death of her step-daughter. Oedipus was saved by a shepherd. The dwarves who lived in the forest saved Snow White, who apparently had been killed by a woodsman. In other children's stories, such as "Red Riding Hood" or "Sleeping Beauty," filicide is to be executed by the Big Bad Wolf or the Evil Witch.

What calls our attention is that such terrible events, as filicide, do not terrify children, who listen to these fables peacefully as entertainment. We must conclude then that, from a very tender age, children unconsciously know that it is something natural, a fact of life.

In Shakespeare's "Romeo and Juliet," I believe the suicide of the lovers to be their parents' pathological filicide, for they are the true responsible parties in their children's tragedy. The same is true in Camilo Castelo Branco's *Amor de Perdição* [Love of Perdition].

Euripides' "Medea" and Dostoyevsky *Brothers Karamazov* are other examples among so many that beautifully and artfully illustrate the perpetration of filicide in human history.

Pathological filicide is very common in religion, too, both in the so-called civilized nations and in tribal rituals. To this day, we still see manifestations amid more primitive populations and in black magic sessions. There is always a god that demands the death of a child. Actually, the first expressions of filicide were found in religion, when parents sacrificed their children for the gods in exchange for good crops, not to mention the Greek Theogony, in which the first gods would bury their children alive, or even swallow them, as Uranus and Cronus did when creating the world before Zeus came along.

The most explicit case of pathological filicide is found in the Old Testament of the Bible. In Abraham's history, God himself demands that the Patriarch sacrifice his one and only child, Isaac, which both obediently accept. It is narrated in the Bible in *Genesis*, the first book of Moses' Pentateuch:

Now it came to pass after these things that God tested Abraham, and said to him, "Abraham!"

And he said, "Here I am."

Then He said, "Take now your son, your only son Isaac, whom you love, and go to the land of Moriah, and offer him there as a burnt offering on one of the mountains of which I shall tell you."

So Abraham rose early in the morning and saddled his donkey, and took two of his young men with him, and Isaac his son; and he split the wood for the burnt offering, and arose and went to the place of which God had told him. Then on the third day Abraham lifted his eyes and saw the place afar off. And Abraham said to his young men, "Stay here with the donkey; the lad and I will go yonder and worship, and we will come back to you."

So Abraham took the wood of the burnt offering and laid it on Isaac his son; and he took the fire in his hand, and a knife, and the two of them went together.

But Isaac spoke to Abraham his father and said, "My father!"

And he said, "Here I am, my son."

Then he said, "Look, the fire and the wood, but where is the lamb for a burnt offering?"

And Abraham said, "My son, God will provide for Himself the lamb for a burnt offering."

So the two of them went together.

Then they came to the place of which God had told him. And Abraham built an altar there and placed the wood in order; and he bound Isaac his son and laid him on the altar, upon the wood. And Abraham stretched out his hand and took the knife to slay his son.

But the Angel of the Lord called to him from heaven and said, "Abraham, Abraham!"

So he said, "Here I am."

And He said, "Do not lay your hand on the lad, or do anything to him; for now I know that you fear God, since you have not withheld your son, your only son, from Me."

Then Abraham lifted his eyes and looked, and there behind him was a ram caught in a thicket by its horns. So Abraham went and took the ram, and offered it up for a burnt offering instead of his son.

Then the Angel of the Lord called to Abraham a second time out of heaven, and said: "By Myself I have sworn, says the Lord, because you have done this thing, and have not withheld your son, your only son; I will bless you, and I will multiply your descendants as the stars of the heaven and as the sand which is on the seashore; and your descendants shall possess the gate of their enemies. In your seed all the nations of the earth shall be blessed, because you have obeyed My voice." So Abraham returned to his young men, and they rose and went together to Beersheba; and Abraham dwelt at Beersheba.

(Genesis, 21-22)

Undoubtedly, it was a drastic proof that Jehovah demanded of Abraham when testing his faith to make him the Father of the chosen people. In fact, he did not commit filicide, but we can understand from the story that it would be possible and normal and that Jehovah is an authoritarian and absolute Lord to whom everything can be sacrificed, including the life of a son, who is the property of his father, who in turn is the property of God.

Faithful to its origins, the Jewish religion only worships Jehovah, the one and only God. There is no Son of God in Judaism, He who comes to redeem all sins in the world, as we see in Christian religions, nor is there Prophet Muhammad, the facilitator between Allah and Islamic believers. As in the Old Testament, in which Jehovah resolved the problems faced by the Jewish people directly, to this day the people of Israel continue to have no facilitators between them and God. Maybe it is due to the highly prosecuting environment of Judaism that the promised Messiah is yet to be born. Therefore, they lack the mercy of Christ as a Savior (Christianity), and the kindness of the Mother of God and the protective intervention of Saints (Catholicism). Their God remains distant, as unreachable as before, when it was not allowed to the "chosen people" to utter His sacred name, which was replaced with "Jehovah".

For me, in addition to "filicide" in the form of mandatory circumcision, the Jewish people still commits the most severe form of filicide by not even allowing the birth of the Messiah who had been promised to them by God throughout their history, thus the very reason why they exist as the "chosen people."

On the other hand, Christianity has the most noteworthy and sacred execution of filicide. According to the Bible, in the *Book of Genesis* of the Old Testament[62], everything started when the first parents of humanity, Adam and Eve, were driven from Paradise by God after they ate the forbidden fruit from the "Tree of Knowledge of Good and Evil." They had explicitly disobeyed God by committing a sin.[63] "(...) Then their eyes were opened, and they both realized that they were naked." At that moment, they reached a depressive position, finding wisdom and knowledge of a total object, consequently seeing each other as individuals. And God symbolically commits filicide by condemning them to suffering and hard work ("By the sweat of your brow you shall eat bread,") taking back the gift of immortality and restricting their access to the "Tree of Life".[64]

However, the most noteworthy act of filicide was

---

62 The Old Testament contains traditions that date back to ancient times. It is not a true history book, not even of natural history, whose purpose is to expose the origins of the world and humanity. However, despite the creative and popular contents therein, its teachings are deep and profound: God created the world and is separate from the universe.

63 Even though the popular belief is that Adam and Eve's sin is of a sexual nature, Christian religions associate it with pride: "Your eyes will be opened and you will be like Gods (...)" the serpent told Eve. When the woman saw that the fruit of the tree was good for food and pleasing to the eye, and also desirable for gaining wisdom, she took some and ate it."

64 The tree with the forbidden fruit was the Tree of Life: "And the Lord God said, 'Man has now become like one of us, knowing good and evil. He must not be allowed to reach out his hand and take also from the tree of life and eat, and live forever.' So the Lord God banished him from the Garden of Eden (...) and placed (...) cherubim and a flaming sword flashing back and forth to guard the way to the tree of life."

yet to come. In order to redeem Humanity from the original sin—disobedience inherited from the original parents—, Christians recognizes Jesus as the Messiah promised to the chosen people.

For Christians, God (or Jehovah for the Israelites) is part of the Holy Trinity (Father, Son, and the Holy Ghost), being personified by his own Son (Jesus, son of Maria, from the tribe of David, with the Holy Ghost). That is when God commits His main act of filicide. Jesus is the Messiah and fulfills all prophecies found in the Old Testament, but God sacrifices him in the most painful way, under torture and humiliation. "My God, why have you forsaken me?!" Christ cries out from the cross.

Portuguese author José Saramago wrote a novel called *The Gospel According to Jesus Christ* to explore this issue from the perspective of Jesus as a common man who, by fits and starts, understands his mission as the Messiah.

> Jesus realized then that he had been tricked, as the lamb led to sacrifice is tricked, and that his life had been planned for death from the very beginning. Remembering the river of blood and suffering that would flow from his side and flood the globe, he called out to the open sky, where God could be seen smiling, Men, forgive Him, for He knows not what He has done. Then he began expiring in the midst of a dream (...).[65]

And so, Saramago turned the original words of Christ around ("Father, forgive them, for they know not

---

65 SARAMAGO, José. *O Evangelho segundo Jesus Cristo.* São Paulo: Companhia das Letras, 1991. P 444.

what they have done!") to establish the greatest filicide, that of God against his only son, Jesus Christ. With Abraham, the All-Powerful God suspended Isaac's sacrifice just in time, but filicide was consummated with Jesus, albeit compensated gloriously in the Resurrection of the Christ, an important dogma upon which Christian religions are actually founded.

Combining History and Religion, there are several other reports of children being slaughtered. Moses, circa 1200 b.C., was rescued from a water craft adrift down the river to escape a Pharaoh's decree, who ordered the death of all male babies born to Hebrew parents enslaved in Egypt. His intention was to exterminate them (genocide). In the early 1st century, King Herod of Judea feared competition from the Messiah, whom he knew had already been born, and ordered the death of all children under two years of age living in the region. Before History, Greek mythology symbolically depicted the essence of Men and had rich examples of actual filicide: Gods who kill, order the death, or mutilate their children.

Ultimately, after so many millennia, filicide remains alive among men in diversified forms, as reported by the media: Wars, crimes, abandonment and omission. These are not mere fantasies, as we could have concluded from literary works. The material is broad and abundant, common to the field of Sociology and individual human behavior.

In no way can this subject be overlooked in psychoanalysis, in which I believe filicide remains a taboo, considering the few authors who have addressed it, despite the severe consequences that it brings to the development of the human mind. It is up to us, professionals working in this area, to study the subject more deeply in order to prevent and treat these painful and discriminated mental illnesses.

Omnipotence vs. Impotence in Psychosis

Omnipotence is a false power that people feel that they have, which can lead them to carry an excess of emotion. When this excess becomes unbearable, any individual will present symptoms of illness, either in the mental or the somatic spheres. When talking to my patients, I use expressions such as "You're feeling all-powerful" or "You're taking it all in so silently until you get blue in the face." The fact is that omnipotence exists with or without the illness.

The word "omnipotence" is used indiscriminately in psychology offices when it comes to treating psychotic patients. However, during my clinical work I have noticed that there are two very different types of omnipotence, and one of these types should actually have a different name.

1. Omnipotence vs. Impotence

There is the omnipotence of patients who, in order not to feel their *impotence*, unconsciously pretend to be strong enough to "hold down the fort." We can work this feeling of impotence with patients, which is what makes them feel so superior to any event, capable of everything, and ready to face anything because they think they can take the emotion *without seeing their ego crumbling down*. Actually, if these patients are understood correctly by the therapist and can experience their real impotence, they'll be able to reach their true potential, because *they will have an ego* that is sufficiently together for such a task.

2. Impotence vs. Non-differentiation

There is another kind of patient who is indeed omnipotent, but in the wrong way. They present non-differentiation stages when they lack internalized objects. They actually lack any trace of ego, so much so that their attitudes seem to be omnipotent when what they actually feel is fear. It is similar to a large trash can into which spoiled items are deposited, either by patients themselves or by those around them. This happens because they can't make a distinction between what belongs to themselves and what belongs to others. To them, the *Other* doesn't exist and they accept and incorporate everything as if it were their own. There is no ego to set the boundaries of a field where it is Me vs. Other. It's like adding a drop of water to an amoeba. It will stretch itself and incorporate that drop of water as a part of itself in the utmost manifestation of impotence. *However, there's no omnipotence as an offset to impotence.* Patients feel squashed by a commotion of emotions and they don't know to whom these emotions belong or from where they are coming.

We, the therapists, cannot mistake the omnipotence/impotence of those who have traces of ego—even an integrated ego, as that of the so-called "normal" people—for the impotence/ non-differentiation of those who have no ego at all. In sum, there is the omnipotence/impotence of those who have an ego, despite how disassembled it may be, and the impotence/ non-differentiation of those who are yet to form their ego or, had they formed their ego before, have it undone at the moment. In this case, what matters first is to work with the non-differentiation aspect of it, not with impotence.

Oedipus Complex vs. Depressive Position

When I referred to these emotional development stages in babies throughout this book, I meant to use them as synonyms. Rather, Melanie Klein would have given a new name to Freud's Oedipal phase, by saying that the baby had achieved what she called a "depressive phase" at about nine months. Freud places the Oedipal phase at about five or six years. The fact is that both refer to the same phenomenon, that is, the child's acknowledgement of a father not as a person who is a mere family member, but as the individual performing the *role of father*. The way I see it, this acknowledgement happens in the depressive and/or Oedipal phase, but I disagree with Melanie Klein. Despite her vast experience with children, I do not believe that babies who are nine, ten, or even twelve months old have the emotional and biological potential to acknowledge that man living in their house as the Father (the individual playing the role of father) or the woman nursing them as the Mother (playing the role of mother).

Therefore, considering my long history working

with psychotic patients—which is as extensive as Melanie Klein's history with babies—I can assure that, during their treatment, there is a clear lack of or even inability to form symbols before five or six years of age. This is a crucial requirement for children to acknowledge themselves and their parents as total objects, that is, as individuals invested in their respective roles of father, mother, and child. For psychotic patients going through an adequate treatment, this is the time they take to form or reform their ego and reveal how long it took for them to go through all the transformations they've experienced.

In addition to Freud, there is a habit that comes to my aid, and it is not a gratuitous one. Teachers only teach children how to read or write at around six years of age, and this is not a coincidence. Like me, educators believe that a child's ego is only mature enough when there's a parallel emotional development corresponding to this age, even though there are exceptions.

POSSIBLE TRACES OF LIFE IN UTERO AS SEEN IN PSYCHOSIS[66]

The facts below refer to the behavior of twin patients and other patients who have had the umbilical cord wrapped around their neck while in utero.

When I was working as a psychiatric aide in 1962 at the Pinel Clinic in Porto Alegre, State of Rio Grande do Sul, I met the first set of twins that I'll mention here—there will be six sets in total. These were monozygotic male twins and the crisis of acute schizophrenic psychosis of one of them did not coincide with those of the other. However, I remember that both complained about the same things during their hospitalization, such as "This clinic is too small," or "I'm just half a person." Whenever they were discharged and went back home, they wanted to sleep in bed with their mother, a widow, because their bedroom was "way too big."

In 1966, while working at the same dynamic hospital during my first year of post-graduation studies in Psychiatry, I had the opportunity to treat another set of

66 Presentation for a Study Group in São Paulo, 1990.

monozygotic twins. I was impressed by how similar the circumstances were. They were also the sons of a widow and had suffered psychotic episodes during their adolescence, when their father died. During their psychotic crises, they physically attacked their mother and were hospitalized. To my astonishment, they made the exact same complaints of that first set of twins. Both of them perceived themselves as "half a person, not whole like others." For this reason, they would physically turn against their mother who, according to them, had attacked them before (trying to kill them).

Today, under the light of psychoanalysis, I understood that these twins had shared the space within a single amniotic sac, within the same womb, and felt that the inside world (in utero) was too small, while the world outside was too big for "half" people. Additionally, I realized that these four people reacted aggressively towards their mothers as if she had tried to kill them for having "divided" them in utero. Against this alleged pathological filicide attempt, they rebelled by attacking their respective mothers physically (matricide attempts). I was in Rio de Janeiro between 1969 and 1989, where I had the opportunity to meet another four sets of twins, even though I only treated two of these individuals, and each came from a different set.

The First Set

The first set of twins was no longer a pair while

still in utero. One of the twins, according to the mother, "absorbed" the other and became fat and strong. The truth is that there was no Other, which didn't develop and was not born. They don't know if the "absorbed" sibling was a male or female, but there is a possibility that they were monozygotic twins, which would allow for the "absorption."

The mother did not allow the child that was born to develop himself emotionally and treated him as an incapable individual. He became a criminal. He committed homicide, maybe even more. I say "more" because the mother omitted anything that could incriminate that fellow, who couldn't get a steady job or lead a normal life.

Today, I believe that patient felt he had killed his brother in the womb and reproduced the event in the outside world by committing homicide. This fact is interesting because, on the one hand, he felt he was a murderer, but on the other he was sure that his mother did not approve him.

The Second Set

In the second set of twins, which were truly monozygotic, the same case is repeated almost identically. One of the twins ended up alone. During his very first appointment, in 1985, he told me right away, "Doctor, I'm homicidal." I must have shown that I was shocked, because right away he added, "I killed my twin brother, the other one, in my mother's womb."

I asked him if he was seeking treatment because he wanted to kill himself as well. He said that was one of the reasons, the other one being that he was afraid he could kill his younger brother, a teenager. The mother confirmed the death of the twin in utero. The patient had learned about that fact by chance, as an adult. Why had the mother omitted the truth? Did she think he was homicidal and she herself was filicidal? After talking to her, I confirmed that the patient had indeed attacked his younger brother, and the mother did not dare interfere with their fights. By acting this way, she emphasized the homicidal idea that her son had of himself, so that he wouldn't think that she had been the one who killed the other twin in utero. One was putting the blame on the other.

Sometimes, my patient would attack the mother, saying that she had killed his brother, but many other timed he was the one who was afraid of being killed by her. He attempted suicide several times.

The Third Set

This was a set of dizygotic female twins. One of them, the ugly one, became mentally ill. The other one, the pretty one, committed suicide abruptly without anyone noticing her illness.

The Fourth Set

Regarding the filicidal behavior of parents, I remember that only one of the individuals was schizophrenic in this monozygotic set of twins. When the clinic staff warned the mother that her son's life was at risk, she would say, "That's okay, he can kill himself. I have another son just like him back home, and he's healthy." Of course she interrupted the patient's treatment. And the young man committed suicide.

Every single one of these mothers of twin children were super protective and, contradictorily and concomitantly, they were abandoning mothers as well. They all acted very similarly in their role of mother. They didn't allow their children to develop. In a way, they instilled in them the feeling of inability and fratricide, as long as it wouldn't interfere with her behavior, while guiding them towards a healthy behavior. Apparently, these twins loved their respective mothers and carried the burden of this filicidal, suicidal, homicidal, and matricidal connection, becoming unhappy and useless, even dangerous to society.

As far as the cord wrapped around the neck, I met six people at the clinic I used to work at who had been born under these circumstances, which allows me to assume that they had an agitated, if not disturbed life in utero. There was this time when, "without thinking," I said to one of these patients, "You already wanted to kill yourself in your mother's womb, didn't you?" I only realized the weight of this "joke" later on.

The six patients had been treated at the aforementioned hospital after severe suicide attempts and I was yet to consciously connect the dots. Well, according to Freud's theory of Repetition Compulsion, suicide attempts in these cases were nothing but a repetition of the death experience they had had in utero. Two of them came from families with a history of drug addiction and were drug addicts as well, which made me think that the mother's state must have interacted with the fetus in utero. In fact, one of them had his treatment interrupted and hanged himself. The situation in utero was repeated.

These reports emphasize the idea that events taking place in utero may remain in the fetus' mnemic traces and can potentially be experienced after birth. Or, according to Freud, they can be repeated and acted out. It is up to us, therapists, to know how to work with this material.

Final Considerations[67]

After becoming aware of Piontelli's work,[68] I was able to go beyond my reflections.[69] There was, in fact, fetus suffering in the cases described here.

On the other hand, Piontelli talks about childhood amnesia. Regarding this subject, I wonder if schizophrenics can have amnesia, since one must first have had memory in order to forget. According to Bion, psychotic individuals use repression very little. Well, repression is a basic defense mechanism in emotional development, which is necessary and earlier than memory. In any case, the unconscious mind is timeless and I allow myself to think that schizophrenic individuals have never suffered from amnesia to a degree that would omit complete facts and emotions from their memory. They can only retain pieces of events, because they only have traces of mem-

67 Originally written in 1993.
68 Alessandra Piontelli is an associate member of the Italian Psychoanalytic Society and works as a child neuropsychiatrist and psychotherapist.
69 I read Piontelli's work in 1993 and this presentation took place in 1990.

ories available to them upon retaining very little of what they have incorporated. For them, everything is happening "now," the moment when mnemic traces are registered. Consequently, what we see as "delusional ideas" or "hallucinations" may as well be the manifestation of mnemic traces of what has indeed taken place and was experienced during precocious childhood or life in utero, facts that have occurred, were properly experienced, or simply captured by the parents' unconscious mind.

I thought the report of these clinical observations should be part of a book on filicide. I trust readers to seek a deeper understanding of their meaning.

BIBLIOGRAPHICAL REFERENCES

BION, W. R. *Volviendo A Pensar*. Buenos Aires: Ediciones Horme S.A.E., Editorial Paidos, 1966.

BRANDÃO, Junito de Souza. *Mitologia Grega*. Petrópolis: Editora Vozes, 1986.

COHEN, Mortimer J. *Caminhos da Bíblia*. Rio de Janeiro: Editora Tradição, 1967.

DAMETTO, Carmem. *O Psicótico e seu Tratamento*. Petrópolis: KBR, 2012.

_____. *Personalidade Psicótica e Psicose*. Rio de Janeiro: Cooperativa dos Profissionais de Imprensa do Est. do Rio de Janeiro, 1981.

_____. *Psicoterapia do Paciente Psicótico*. Petrópolis: KBR, 2012.

_____. *Loucura: Mitos e Realidade*. Petrópolis: KBR, 2012.

FREUD, S. *Obras Completas*. Rio de Janeiro: Editora Delta, 1958.

GRINBERG, Leon. *Culpa e Depressão*. Buenos Aires: Editora Paidos, 1963.

KLEIN, Melanie. *Contribuições à Psicanálise*. São Paulo: Editora Mestre Jou, 1981.

MARTUSCELLO, Carmine. *Suicídio - Percepção e Prevenção*. Rio de Janeiro: Editora Cultura Médica, 1993.

RASCOVSKY, Arnaldo. *O Assassinato dos Filhos (filicídio)*. Rio de Janeiro: Editora Documentário, 1973.

ROSENFELD, H. *Impasse and Interpretation*. Londres: Tavistock, 1987.

_____. *Os Estados Psicóticos*. Rio de Janeiro: Zahar, 1968.

SEGAL, Hanna. *Introdução à obra de Melanie Klein*. Rio de Janeiro: Imago Editora, 1966.

TRACTENBERG, Moisés. "A Taunatofilia Humana". In: *Psicanálise da Circuncisão*. Rio de Janeiro: Editora Civilização Brasileira, 1977.

WINNICOTT, D. W. *O brincar e a realidade*. Rio de Janeiro: Imago, 1975.

_____. *Da Pediatria à Psicanálise*. Rio de Janeiro: Editora Francisco Alves, 1978.

_____. *O Ambiente e os Processos de Maturação*. Porto Alegre: Editora Artes Médicas Sul, 1978.

Discography

BETHÂNIA, Maria. "Nossos Momentos". Rio de

Janeiro: Universal Music/ Philips/ Polygram, 1982.

VELOSO, Caetano. "Muito (dentro da estrela azulada)". Rio de Janeiro: Universal Music/ Philips/ Polygram, 1978.

Printed in Great Britain
by Amazon